101
THINGS
YOU DIDN'T
KNOW ABOUT
Da Vinci

101 THINGS

YOU DIDN'T KNOW ABOUT

Da Vinci

The Secrets of the World's Most Eccentric
and Innovative Genius Revealed!

SHANA PRIWER
&
CYNTHIA PHILLIPS, PH.D.

Adams Media
Avon, Massachusetts

To our children, Zoecyn, Elijah, and Benjamin

Copyright © 2005, F+W Publications, Inc. All rights reserved. This book, or parts thereof, may not be reproduced in any form without permission from the publisher; exceptions are made for brief excerpts used in published reviews.

Published by Adams Media, an F+W Publications Company
57 Littlefield Street, Avon, MA 02322
www.adamsmedia.com.

ISBN: 1-59337-346-5

Printed in Canada.

J I H G F E D C B A

Library of Congress Cataloging-in-Publication Data

This publication is designed to provide accurate and authoritative information with regard to the subject matter covered. It is sold with the understanding that the publisher is not engaged in rendering legal, accounting, or other professional advice. If legal advice or other expert assistance is required, the services of a competent professional person should be sought.
—From a *Declaration of Principles* jointly adopted by a Committee of the American Bar Association and a Committee of Publishers and Associations

Many of the designations used by manufacturers and sellers to distinguish their products are claimed as trademarks. Where those designations appear in this book and Adams Media was aware of a trademark claim, the designations have been printed with initial capital letters.

This book is available at quantity discounts for bulk purchases.
For information, please call 1-800-872-5627.

Contents

Part 6: THE WRITING ON THE WALL ∙ 193

Introduction

Everyone's heard of Leonardo da Vinci—he painted the *Mona Lisa*, he was the first Renaissance man, and didn't he write in some kind of code? But there's much more to Leonardo than that! Did you know that he was one of the first people to make detailed anatomical drawings? Or that he designed one of the first robots? Leonardo da Vinci was not only an amazing artist, he was also a talented scientist, inventor, and musician. Was there anything he wasn't good at? Indeed, Leonardo rarely failed at anything—except he did have a problem finishing what he started!

Leonardo came from less than extraordinary beginnings. He was born in 1452, to a young unmarried couple in the Tuscany region of Italy. Both his parents married other people and eventually had seventeen more children, but none of Leonardo's half siblings went on to become particularly famous. Clearly, Leonardo was special.

By the time he was sixteen, Leonardo's artistic talents were becoming obvious, and his father apprenticed him to a leading artist in Florence. When Leonardo painted a small angel in one of his boss's paintings, he did such a good job that his master supposedly took one look and swore he'd give up painting forever! Leonardo certainly knew how to make an impression.

Throughout his long career, Leonardo worked for everyone from kings and dukes to warlords. He wasn't just a painter, either—he traveled as a military engineer with the infamous Cesare Borgia, using his genius to create machines of war. During more peaceful times, Leonardo was fond of making mathematical discoveries, investigating the secrets of the human body, and inventing parachutes. In his spare time, he even came up with plans to divert an entire river!

In spite of these endeavors, Leonardo is mostly famous today for his paintings, though only a handful of his finished works survive. Leonardo started countless projects, but finished only a few. Even the paintings he did manage to finish suffered from his constant innovation. In fact, most of Leonardo's inventions weren't ever built—he would come up with an amazing design, work on it for a while, and then when he was satisfied that it might work (or was just plain bored), he'd move on to something else. Luckily for us, Leonardo wrote about these unfinished projects in his detailed notebooks.

Even during the Renaissance, it was clear that Leonardo was a genius. But when we look at his accomplishments today, the breadth of his talents is even more remarkable. Not only did he paint one of the most amazing and talked-about paintings of all time, the *Mona Lisa*, he came up with designs for a helicopter, a mechanical loom, a car, a bicycle, and a multi-barreled gun!

Leonardo really is the definition of a Renaissance man: He was not just good at what he did, he was a groundbreaking innovator. Many of his designs would have revolutionized society if they'd been built during his time. Of course, that was one of Leonardo's biggest problems—he was ahead of his time. Although it would have been impossible to build many of his inventions with the limited resources available during the Renaissance, when models have been built in modern times, they've worked perfectly. Imagine what he could have accomplished with modern technology!

Fasten your seatbelts, sit back, relax, and enjoy this tour through the phenomenal accomplishments of one of the most amazing people ever to live!

Part 1

IN THE BEGINNING

One of the Renaissance's favorite sons had a less-than-spectacular start in life. Born the illegitimate son of a notary and a peasant girl in a small town near Florence, Italy, Leonardo da Vinci soon rose to fame as no one else could (or did). His family, his surroundings in the Tuscan countryside, and the time of his birth all influenced Leonardo's formative years—the early years of the burgeoning Italian Renaissance.

Because of his illegitimate birth, Leonardo didn't have to follow in his father's footsteps. He was able to spend much of his childhood studying exactly what he wanted, rather than what he was told to; he spent years looking at and drawing the world around him. Later, Leonardo's apprenticeship in Andrea Verrocchio's workshop had an enormous impact on his artistic and scientific works. Once he "graduated" to doing his own projects, he incorporated many of the Renaissance's rapidly evolving themes. At the time Leonardo entered Verrocchio's workshop, Florence was the hub of a bustling new world of intellectual expression, trade, banking, and other innovations. As Europe burst out of the stagnant Middle Ages into a flowering period full of promise, Leonardo da Vinci was at the center.

Where it all began: Vinci, Italy

Every good story has an eventful beginning, and this one begins with the birth of a child named Leonardo in Italy, on April 15, 1452. In those days, it was customary for Renaissance Italians to take the name of their birth city as part of their full identification. And so Leonardo, by virtue of being born in Vinci, was known as Leonardo da Vinci (Leonardo from Vinci).

Vinci is located about fifty kilometers to the west of Florence, deep in the Tuscany region. Vinci is also near Pisa (home of the famed Leaning Tower), as well as Siena and Lucca. Long before the Renaissance, Vinci was home to the Etruscans and contained many ancient castles, including the Castello Guidi (built for the Conti Guidi during the Middle Ages). The town's rolling green countryside must have been a source of inspiration for Leonardo's budding artistic talent. Surrounded by such beauty, who wouldn't be moved to draw it?

However, not everyone thinks Leonardo actually came from Vinci. One theory holds Leonardo was actually born in Anchiano, a town located about three kilometers from Vinci. Why? For one thing, Da Vinci's family supposedly lived there. Anchiano also boasts a farmhouse that many people think is where Leonardo first entered this world, fittingly nicknamed the Casa Natale di Leonardo (which literally means "the birth house of Leonardo"). Today, the farmhouse is home to a permanent exhibit of Leonardo's drawings and other works. Restored in the mid-1980s, the house is decorated with many of Leonardo's landscape paintings—so if nothing else, it's a great place to see Leonardo's work!

Even if Leonardo was actually born in Anchiano, he clearly spent much of his childhood in Vinci. Vinci today is the home of the Leonardo Museum, which occupies part of the Castello dei Conti Guidi. The castle was converted into a museum in 1953 to celebrate the 500th anniversary of Leonardo's birth. The main exhibit includes some of Leonardo's machine designs and models, including cranes, winches, clocks, and helicopters.

Sketches, notes, sculptures, and other descriptions of how the machines might have worked accompany them.

In addition to this museum, there are other points of interest in Vinci. It's home to the Santa Croce Church, which boasts Leonardo's rumored baptismal font. A new museum is also being planned; this facility will be devoted to Leonardo's paintings, as a complement to the existing museum, which focuses on his inventions.

Modern-day Vinci continues to hold yearly festivals that celebrate Leonardo and his artistic legacy. Today, the town is home to about 14,000 people.

The mamas and the papas, and everyone in between

As explained in this book's introduction, Leonardo's parents were not married. Aside from that, who were these people who gave birth to one of the greatest artistic minds of all time? His mother, Caterina, was a sixteen-year-old peasant girl; his father, twenty-five-year-old Ser Piero di Antonio, was a notary. A wedding was forbidden between the two young lovers because of their class difference, and Ser Piero was quickly married off to a more appropriate mate, Albiera. Caterina also married a few months after Leonardo's birth.

Like Leonardo himself, his mother led a life of mystery. She may have been a slave of Middle Eastern ancestry. Slave ownership was common in Tuscany at that time, and slaves who had converted to Christianity from Eastern, pagan, or Jewish religions often took the name Caterina. It's even possible that Caterina was Ser Piero's slave!

While Ser Piero's father was a farmer, Ser Piero's family included lots of notaries. At that time, the position of notary was similar to a lawyer, and Ser Piero had a relatively privileged position in society. Because he was illegitimate, though, Leonardo shared none of his father's privilege. Even if he'd wanted to, he couldn't have followed in his father's footsteps. Luckily, this turned out to be the best thing that could have happened! Leonardo was free to pursue life as an artist.

Although we don't know much about Leonardo's early days, we do know his father wasn't rich enough to afford a wet nurse. Consequently, Leonardo probably lived with his mother during his first few years so that she could nurse him. Then, somewhere between the age of three and five, Leonardo went to live with his father and step-mother. Notes from Leonardo's grandfather Antonio show that five-year-old Leonardo was living with his father at his grandfather's house in 1457. But Leonardo spent little time with Ser Piero, who was often away on business in Florence.

So who affected Leonardo as a child? It seems that his greatest influence was his uncle Francesco. (Leonardo and his uncle were so close that Francesco even remembered him in his will.) Ser Piero's brother Francesco was a farmer, and when Leonardo was with him, he would have gotten to spend quite a bit of time outside. While he probably had to help tend to the animals, he would have also had time to observe and sketch nature and landscapes.

Both Caterina and Ser Piero had a number of other children, eventually leaving Leonardo with a whopping seventeen half brothers and sisters: twelve children from his father and five from his mother. Now that is one big extended family! The births of these other children were spread out over the years—Ser Piero's first legitimate son was born twenty-four years after Leonardo's birth, which explains why Leonardo was treated as a legitimate son of Ser Piero's household.

Caterina remained in the Vinci area for most of her life, although she came to live with Leonardo in Milan in 1493. She resided there with her son, until her death in 1495.

"Current events" in fifteenth-century Italy

Even before Leonardo's birth, pre-Renaissance Italy was gearing up for a dramatic shift from the Middle Ages. While most of the heavy hitters were yet to come, Italy was rapidly becoming a hot spot for invention and innovation. Many of the world's best-known artists rose to fame in the years before Leonardo, and their efforts made Leonardo's own success possible.

Historically speaking, fourteenth-century Italy was a mishmash of city-states. Italy still had a long way to go before it would become a single, united country—this unification didn't occur until the mid-nineteenth century. Small political groups were constantly battling each other, leading to a fairly unstable atmosphere. Feudalism, a two-tiered system of lords and peasants, provided yet another reason for discontent. Do you think such hostility would have made it impossible for artists to break out with new styles? Not at all—artists were actually responsible for helping to reshape Western European society. Dante, Giotto, Brunelleschi, Alberti, and later Leonardo were all artists who created a cultural connection between feudalism's two class extremes.

Let's take a quick look at some of these pre-Renaissance masters. Fillipo Brunelleschi (1377–1446) was one of Florence's primary architects and sculptors in the 100 or so years before Leonardo da Vinci's rise to fame. As a young architect, Brunelleschi was known for combining elements of classical architecture with designs that reflected the Renaissance's rising sense of independence and freedom. His major projects included the cathedral of Santa Maria del Fiore, the cupola of the Duomo, and the Ospedale degli Innocenti, all in Florence. In 1401, Brunelleschi, along with Florentine sculptor, painter, and goldsmith Lorenzo Ghiberti, won a competition to create the doors of the Duomo Baptistery. (The baptistery is one of the buildings that makes up the Florence Duomo cathedral complex.) Leonardo's life paralleled Brunelleschi's in many ways. Like Leonardo, Brunelleschi was first trained in metalsmithing and sculpture. He was apprenticed early in his career, so he was able to learn new skills while honing existing ones. Also like Leonardo, Brunelleschi sketched throughout his life, including designs for different machines and platforms. He was perhaps the most prolific architect of the day, and his multifaceted approach to art and science was a great source of inspiration to Leonardo.

Leone Batista Alberti (1404–1472) was another Italian architect who helped set the stage for Leonardo. Alberti was one of the earliest Italian artists to include perspective and architectural design elements in his painting. He studied in Bologna and Padua and, like Brunelleschi, nurtured an interest in classicism. Alberti's main contribution to the pre-Renaissance era was his intense fascination with geometry. He was one of the first architects to incorporate mathematical structure into construction, interpreting three-dimensional forms as a system of proportions. His major design tasks included the Chapel Rucellai and the façade of Santa Maria Novella, both in Florence, and Sant' Andrea in Mantua.

As Italy climbed out of the medieval darkness during the Renaissance, other aspects of Italian culture began to flourish, too. Dante Alighieri (1245–1321), for example, was one of this period's most creative authors, contributing such masterpieces as *The Divine Comedy*, which helped to standardize the Italian language (similar to what Chaucer's *Canterbury Tales* did for English).

Giotto (Ambrogio Bondone, 1267–1337) was perhaps the best-known painter of the thirteenth century. Although he had a background in the Byzantine tradition, Giotto gave it up in exchange for more natural, flowing lines. Giotto is also credited with breathing life back into the art of painting: he modernized both its purpose and aesthetic, and created the illusion of 3-D space on a 2-D canvas. These changes made art more popular and revived a flagging interest in artwork. This artistic revival worked itself into the eventual frenzy of the Renaissance.

The life you're born into

Leonardo's illegitimate status wasn't much of a secret: You could see it simply by examining his name. Officially, he should have been Leonardo di Ser Piero da Vinci, meaning, "Leonardo son of Ser Piero from Vinci." However, Leonardo didn't use his father's name, as was the custom of the time; he referred to himself only as Leonardo da Vinci and signed many of his works just plain Leonardo. By shortening his name even more, he was probably rebelling against his lack of official status and trying to make his own place in the world.

As an illegitimate child, Leonardo's place in the Tuscany region's highly stratified society was, at best, precarious. Class status was important, especially in the new middle classes. In the upper classes, illegitimate children could inherit property and social status from their fathers. The middle classes were sticklers for proper birth and parentage, though; as the illegitimate son of a peasant woman (and possible slave), Leonardo's status was quite low. While the upper classes in the Renaissance were probably secure enough in their status to accept illegitimate children, those in the middle class likely felt that what they had gotten could just as easily be taken away. So middle class folks were much more obsessed with status and would have made it clear that an illegitimate child like Leonardo wasn't really welcome in their ranks.

Even though Leonardo's father raised Leonardo in his household, his illegitimacy disqualified him from the clubs and guilds to which his father belonged. In fact, Leonardo couldn't get a university education, and as mentioned in number 2, he certainly wouldn't have been able to follow in his father's footsteps and become a notary. While his father most likely provided a basic education in reading and writing, Leonardo did much of his learning independently. Eventually, he would teach himself Latin, mathematics, human anatomy, and physics!

With no expectations, Leonardo was free to grow into his full intellect. Because he was not obligated to follow a specific, predefined role, he was able to explore and develop his talents, without anyone pushing him to be something he didn't want to be. His early days on his Uncle Francesco's farm left him with a deep love and respect for nature, as well as a sense of wonder. Through these experiences, he also discovered his talent for drawing and art.

A career as a court artist was one of the most respected occupations that an illegitimate child could hope to achieve. Perhaps Leonardo's father had this in the back of his mind when he apprenticed his son to one of the most respected artists in Florence, Andrea Verrocchio. In any case, it's lucky for us that Leonardo's father had the presence of mind to start him off on such an appropriate path.

Siblings of a genius

Although Leonardo was the first child for both of his parents, as previously mentioned in number 2, he ended up with seventeen half siblings. Leonardo's father was never married to his mother, but he married four other women over the course of his life. This propensity for multiple weddings was one characteristic that Leonardo did not inherit from his father. Ser Piero's first two wives, Albiera and Francesca, both died young and bore no children. His third wife, Margherita, gave birth to two sons, Antonio (Ser Piero's first legitimate heir) in 1476 and Giuliomo in 1479. A girl, Maddalena, was born in 1477, but she died in 1480. Soon after her death, Ser Piero married his fourth wife, Lucrezia, who gave birth to two daughters and seven more sons: Lorenzo in 1484, Violante in 1485, Domenico in 1486, Margherita in 1491, Benedetto in 1492, Pandolfo in 1494, Guglielmo in 1496, Bartolomeo in 1497, and Giovanni in 1498. Leonardo wound up with nine half brothers and two half sisters on his father's side alone. Quite an extended family! In spite of his many options, Leonardo wasn't particularly close to any of his half siblings. By the time Leonardo's first half-brother, Antonio, was born, Leonardo was already twenty-four and a working artist.

Not much is known about the five children that Leonardo's mother, Caterina, had after she was married. These children included three half sisters and one half brother (nothing is known about the fifth), who were closer in age to Leonardo than his father's other children. Records show that two of Caterina's daughters were named Piera (born in 1455) and Maria (born in 1458), and Leonardo notes in his writings that his half brother on his mother's side died from a mortar shot at Pisa. These other kids probably contributed to the distance between Leonardo and his mother. Once Leonardo moved into his father's house, Caterina most likely devoted all her time to her legitimate children, with little to spare for poor Leonardo.

After Ser Piero's death in 1504, Leonardo's half brothers got greedy over their father's property. There was much in-fighting, and Leonardo had to return to Florence a number of times to settle disputes. Apparently, Ser Piero died without a will—not very good planning for a lawyer—which basically led to a feeding frenzy among his offspring. One of Leonardo's half brothers had become a notary like his father, and he took charge of the legal proceedings. He first challenged Leonardo's right to inherit from his father's estate, and then when Ser Piero's brother Francesco died a few years later, he objected to their uncle's will as well. He had a good reason to protest—Leonardo was supposed to get a good chunk of land.

While all this was going on, Leonardo wasn't exactly resting on his laurels; he was the court painter to King Louis XII of France (who happened to live in Milan). Leonardo had many paintings to complete, and the king probably wasn't too happy with all these interruptions to Leonardo's work. In fact, both the French king and Charles d'Amboise, among others, wrote letters to the Florentine authorities, asking them to speed up Leonardo's legal battle. These letters didn't have much effect, however, and the lawsuits continued until 1511. Ultimately, Leonardo didn't receive any inheritance from his father's estate, but he emerged from the years of conflict with rights to his Uncle Francesco's farm, land, and money.

Although none of Leonardo's siblings were particularly artistic, he did have a nephew, Pierfrancesco da Vinci (1531–1554), called Pierino, who was a decent sculptor. The son of Leonardo's half brother Bartolomeo, Pierino was apparently a child prodigy and became known as a talented sculptor before his death in Pisa at the age of twenty-three. In spite of his short career, the sixteenth-century art historian Giorgio Vasari dedicated a biography to Pierino, and one of Pierino's sculptures is in the Louvre! Maybe if he'd lived a little longer, Pierino would have shown more of Leonardo's legacy, but unfortunately we'll never know.

It's all relative

As previously discussed, Leonardo da Vinci came from a long line of notaries—the first one in his family was Ser Guido di Ser Michele da Vinci, who lived in Vinci in the fourteenth century. His two sons, Giovanni and Piero, were also notaries, and Piero's son Antonio was Leonardo's grandfather. In a burst of independence, Leonardo's grandfather, Antonio, broke with family tradition and instead became a farmer. He married Leonardo's grandmother, Lucia (born in 1393), who was the daughter of yet another notary. They had three children: Piero, Leonardo's father, born in 1427; Francesco, born in 1435; and Violante, born some time afterwards. Leonardo and his father lived in the same house as Antonio and Lucia for many years, until the family moved to Florence.

Fortunately, Antonio kept detailed records about his family's life. From these notes, we know that Leonardo was baptized into his father's family almost immediately after his birth. Tax records show Leonardo was part of his grandfather's household by the time he was five years old. Leonardo was still living with his father's family when he was seventeen, already a part of Andrea Verrocchio's studio by that time.

As discussed in number 2, Leonardo's Uncle Francesco had a strong influence on his young nephew. Grandpa Antonio's tax information shows that Francesco lived with the family for a time, though the grandfather wasn't generous with his job description; he put that Francesco "stayed home and did nothing."

Eventually, Francesco started a career as a farmer and landowner, following in his father Antonio's footsteps, while Piero became a notary like his grandfather.

Youthful adventures

Most of us start showing signs of our adult personalities as children. Leonardo was, of course, no different. With his childhood games he would flit from one project to the next, yet when projects interested him, Leonardo could spend hours, even days, working on fine details. As you'll read later, these qualities stuck with him throughout his life.

Giorgio Vasari's biography of Leonardo records one example from childhood of the work habits Leonardo became known for as an adult. According to this report, Leonardo's father received a request from a local peasant to decorate a wooden shield, and he decided to give the project to his young son. Leonardo decorated the shield with the face of Medusa, the mythological serpent-headed creature. Rather than painting a pleasant, romanticized version of Medusa, Leonardo gathered various snakes, lizards, and other creatures from outdoors, positioning them in a studio to use as models. After a few days of work, Leonardo's father came to check on his son's progress. He was in for quite a shock! When he walked into the studio, Ser Piero was not only confronted with the shield's grotesque realism, he got hit with the stench of decomposing reptiles. As the story goes, Leonardo had been oblivious to his models' offensive smell, and didn't seem to mind working amidst dead creatures.

Whether or not this story is actually true, it shows Leonardo's penchant for drawing nature accurately began when he was a child. During his youth, Leonardo probably spent hours on end observing nature first-hand and his earliest sketches were studies of landscapes, plants, and animals. In his future artwork, he used these skills to create realistic-looking natural scenes, in both his scenes with human figures and landscape paintings.

Although his illegitimate birth barred Leonardo from most formal education, including university study, his relatives and family friends probably tutored him. Though he seems to have tried studying Latin on his own, Leonardo never learned it very well. Not knowing Latin came with a heavy price, because it effectively prevented Leonardo from studying ancient Roman writings. Although the revival of classical knowledge was a key element of the Renaissance, Leonardo was forced to innovate largely on his own. It's possible that his poor Latin skills inadvertently helped him; he was forced to use his own innovations and thought processes, and he was almost entirely free of precedent. Sometimes, it's not so bad to go your own way!

Much of Leonardo's early work focused on the interplay of light and shadow, and for Leonardo, nature truly was the best teacher. He was particularly interested in margins, such as the line between the beautiful and the grotesque. Rather than drawing or painting only beautiful things, he searched for the unusual: strange hills and rocks, odd animals, and rare plants. He also continued to study and observe humans; the incredible details he added to his drawings of faces and expressions made him stand out from the crowd.

Throughout his career, Leonardo spent a lot of time sketching and painting images of mothers with children. Hundreds of years later, Sigmund Freud theorized these works, while religious in nature, were Leonardo's attempt to deal with being abandoned by his mother at a young age. Maybe this is a stretch, but then again, maybe you *can* see his lack of a true maternal bond in some of his works, like the painting *The Virgin and Child with Saint Anne*. Here, the child is thought to be a self-portrait, while the Virgin and St. Anne might represent Leonardo's mother, Caterina, and his first step-mother, Albiera. Though such interpretations are only theories, they support the possibility that Leonardo's popular religious themes may have had personal underpinnings.

Get to work! Leonardo's early training

Even before he became famous, Leonardo was heavily involved in the arts. Though he was in many ways a typical kid, he was already beginning to break away from the pack. Unfortunately, not many specifics are known about Leonardo's early education, but it's possible to make a few generalizations based on what we do know.

If you grew up in New York, you might have spent hours drawing skyscrapers. In much the same way, Leonardo, who grew up in the beautiful Tuscan countryside, learned to draw by studying the mountainous landscape. He used everything he had available—sketching, painting, and modeling—to record the natural environment. His grandfather's notes mention that Leonardo spent time drawing animals and plants, indicating a keen awareness of the world around him.

Leonardo got a taste for a wide variety of arts at a young age. He studied music and singing during his formative years, learning to play the lyre and other Renaissance instruments. One of his favorite "academic" subjects was probably mathematics; the ability to apply mathematical principles to art would, of course, be one of his signature trademarks later on. Is it possible that Leonardo simply had too much exposure to too many different things as a child? Leonardo was known for starting more tasks than he finished; his notebooks reveal many ideas that never actually took shape. Maybe he tried so many things, he never learned to focus on one at a time.

Perhaps not insignificantly, Leonardo was left-handed. Generally speaking, the right hemisphere of the human brain (more dominant in left-handed people) controls art, music, creativity, and emotions. In contrast, right-handed people are more oriented toward the left hemisphere of the brain, which is associated with math, science, language, and speech. Leonardo's left-handedness likely has something to do with his unusual style of writing, which flowed from right to left. He wrote letters backwards, so they formed a mirror image. You might already know someone who writes this way—this style isn't uncommon among left-handed people, and Leonardo could have devised the technique as a child. Some historians believe he developed it as a sort of secret code to protect his notes and sketchbooks from being copied; others think it was the result of being both left-handed and dyslexic. Whatever the reason, Leonardo's writing method added to his uniqueness and made his homework pretty hard to copy!

During the Renaissance, artists couldn't just run down to the corner art supply store for paints and brushes—they had to make things themselves. As a child, Leonardo probably used materials he found or borrowed from his grandfather to create his sketches. Though only seventeen years old when he was apprenticed to master artist Verrocchio, Leonardo had already shown promise. Few dated drawings survive from Leonardo's childhood and the first few years of his apprenticeship. Nevertheless, one of Leonardo's earliest known drawings, a pen-and-ink landscape of the Arno Valley, from 1473, is also one of the first drawings ever to detail landscape in a truly realistic, convincing style. Even at the beginning of his career, Leonardo was already innovating!

What did they do before there were bookstores?

Leonardo da Vinci's early educational resources were few and far between. He certainly didn't walk to the nearest Borders to pick up new books! Rather, most of his knowledge came from experience. As previously discussed, he spent plenty of time with his Uncle Francesco as a youngster. Being a farmer, Francesco taught Leonardo much about nature. Leonardo's early interest in sketching probably began at this time.

While textbooks and teachers were scarce, Leonardo still loved to read. Though his formal schooling probably didn't go past a primary grade, he took advantage of friends' and relatives' libraries. After moving in with his grandfather, he was probably home-schooled in math, science, reading, and writing. Amazingly, he learned physics and anatomy more or less on his own.

Leonardo certainly wasn't the only artist who didn't go to college. Many others were self-educated, which goes to show that if you want to strike it big, you need to get out there and do what needs to be done. Michelangelo Buonarroti, another one of the Renaissance's greatest artists and architects, didn't have much formal instruction either, but he persevered and ultimately carved his own distinct place in history. Schooling or no schooling, great artists such as Michelangelo and Leonardo quickly gained skill and talent far beyond what most achieve in a lifetime.

Apprenticeship, or learning from your elders

When Leonardo was sixteen (in 1468), his paternal grandfather died and his remaining family moved to Florence. This move would ultimately be of great importance to Leonardo's career; Florence was home to many of the best artists of the day, including Andrea Verrocchio (1435–1488). Art took many forms during the Renaissance, and Verrocchio was not only a master of painting, but also sculpture, goldsmithing, music, and other arts. No doubt, Leonardo's father made a smart move by securing his son an apprenticeship with such a great master.

Florence in the mid-fifteenth century was a haven for up-and-coming artists; imagine a loose parallel to Greenwich Village in New York City. Except in those days, patrons worked more closely with artisans. Artists held high social positions, were well respected, and often mingled with powerful Italian families. By the mid-1470s, Florence was home to more than fifty stoneworking shops and close to thirty master painting studios. For a student like Leonardo, there was no better place to be.

But Leonardo wasn't the only star in the sky. Verrocchio had other students, including Sandro Botticelli. Still, apprenticeship did have its advantages for Leonardo. There was a fairly established program for the skills interns had to learn, and Leonardo studied the technical aspects of painting, including how to grind and mix pigments into various paint colors. He probably also studied color theory, learning which colors combine to form other colors, how saturation could contribute to different tones, and so on. You can't paint if you don't know the fundamentals, and Leonardo certainly learned them well.

This crucial internship covered the basics of painting on wood panels. Leonardo was probably also exposed to canvas techniques, including how to stretch and prepare canvases for painting and how different materials would accept paint in different ways. Leonardo also got his first introduction to casting in bronze, a skill he mastered later on down the road. He certainly learned bronze casting from one of the best—Verrocchio was responsible for some of the greatest bronzes the world had ever seen, such as his *David* and his equestrian statue with Bartolomeo Colleoni. He also created bronzes of many saints, including St. John and St. Peter. In addition to metalworking in 3-D, Verrocchio produced bronze relief sculptures, quite common at the time. To put it in modern terms, Verrocchio's studio was the Harvard of the Renaissance.

Leonardo's apprenticeship in Verrocchio's studio lasted until about 1472.

At that time he was admitted to the Company of Painters, Florence's painting guild. Probably eager to test the waters on his own, Leonardo had the opportunity to branch out as an independent artist. But he didn't give up all ties to Verrocchio's workshop, probably because he wanted to further his education and continue his association with the master.

Collaboration on paintings was not uncommon at this time; a patron might provide the general direction for a piece of art; sometimes entire studios (masters and apprentices) worked together on a single painting. Leonardo assisted Verrocchio with at least one of his great works, *The Baptism of Christ*, in 1472. The two artists also collaborated on other works, including the *Madonna di Piazza* (1474). Though Leonardo must have gradually evolved from a student to an equal in Verrocchio's eyes, he didn't come into his own until he started working alone.

Turning dust into gold: Early painting experience

Leonardo da Vinci probably got his first formal exposure to artists' technical tools during his apprenticeship to Andrea Verrocchio (see number 10). As already mentioned, artists in the fifteenth century had to make their paints from scratch. Leonardo much preferred oil paint because it allowed subtle variations in the colors that just weren't possible with tempera.

The science of mixing oil paints was intense; it certainly wasn't a simple skill. The paint had to be colored, and it also had to adhere properly to the painted surface. Paint is a type of emulsion (a liquid suspension where oil and water are mixed together, suspending the oil in the water). Look closely the next time you reach for a bottle of oil-and-vinegar salad dressing; you'll notice the seasonings floating to the top. That mixture is a suspension. Milk contains lots of fat droplets, which spread out over a glass or bottle; they never fully mix and create another type of suspension called an emulsion. Paint is a colloid, a particular sort of emulsion containing solids (pigment) suspended in a liquid (oil + binders). Complicated stuff, and Leonardo had to learn it well!

In Leonardo's first year at Andrea Verrocchio's shop, he likely worked as a *garzone* (a sort of servant). While he had cleaning and other menial tasks to perform, one of his most important jobs would have been making paint. At the time, pigments came from a variety of natural sources: Plants and minerals provided the greatest variety of colors. Leonardo would have spent hours washing and then hand grinding local Italian minerals. Doesn't sound like much fun, but important work, nevertheless. Iron was a commonly available mineral during this period, as was terra verte (found mostly near Verona, Italy). Renaissance painters didn't have dust masks or any way to keep from inhaling airborne particles; they would just measure an amount of pigment onto their grinding surface, add water into the middle of the pile, then start to grind. And they probably had to be careful not to sneeze!

Color alone isn't enough to make paint; you need to mix it with a medium (like oil or water) that will carry the color and dry along with it. A third substance makes the color adhere to the oil or water. During the Renaissance, most artists used animal products, such as eggs, animal glue, or milk, as binding agents to stick the paint to the wood, canvas, or wall surface. After grinding the pigments into a thick paste, Leonardo would have either added the color and the other requisite ingredients to the oil to make paint to use right away, or else he'd have stored it carefully for later use.

Leonardo improved the technique of creating oil paintings by mixing ground pigments with linseed oil and adding beeswax and water to the paint while it was in a boiling stage; this additive kept the colors light and prevented oversaturation. As you'll see later, some of his painting innovations were more successful than others. More important than the new techniques, though, was the fact that he used oil paint extensively, which caused a ripple effect throughout the artistic community. Given how successful his paintings were, it's not surprising that people wanted to copy his techniques!

In addition to painting, Leonardo almost certainly learned how to make and draw with chalk while apprenticed to Verrocchio. In Renaissance Italy, mineral chalks were dug out of the ground and fashioned into drawing tools. Red and brown chalks (common earth tones) were the most popular, and Leonardo used those most in his later chalk drawings.

Getting off to a good start

Leonardo's period with Verrocchio (1468–1472) was his first foray into professional art. While apprentices often worked with their masters on commissioned projects, most of these students didn't go on to outshine their teachers! Then again, most of the students weren't Leonardo da Vinci, either.

The first real tip-off to Leonardo's talents came when he worked on a painting called *The Baptism of Christ*, completed in 1472. Andrea Verrocchio was the official painter, but Leonardo also took part. The monks from the Florentine church of San Salvi requested the painting, and many members of Verrocchio's studio worked on it. Though apprentices like Leonardo had to do office duty and other routine tasks, they also got to help on the master's jobs. In this painting, Verrocchio probably painted Christ and John the Baptist. Although written documentation is slim, it's thought that Da Vinci did some of the landscape and added a kneeling angel supporting the mantle. This figure appears more lifelike than the others; the angel's expression, hair, and clothing are particularly detailed. The angel in question was also painted in oil, Leonardo's paint of choice, whereas much of the remainder of the painting was done in tempera.

Using diagnostic technology to examine this painting, historians have essentially proved that Verrocchio did a master sketch before applying paint. From these tests, you can see that Leonardo strayed from this overall scheme and took liberties with his portion of the painting. You can also see that Leonardo's rendering of the landscape, full of shadows and bright sunlight, is different from the parts Verrocchio painted. Even at this early point in his career, Leonardo was using his own creativity and invention rather than simply following orders. That kind of attitude worked because he was highly skilled. Still, we'll never know if Verrocchio was angry or pleased with Leonardo's changes to his initial design.

Leonardo often made clay study-models of figures before committing them to canvas or wood. In the case of the angel in this painting, Leonardo probably made a clay model and then painted from the model. This technique might explain the apparent stiffness in the folds of the cloth draping Leonardo's angel, but it speaks volumes about Leonardo's willingness to experiment. And, of course, Leonardo was right—the best way to learn to paint something is to study it in 3-D!

While Verrocchio's work didn't exactly pale in comparison to Leonardo's, it was clear from this early work that Leonardo's painting abilities would eventually surpass those of his master. In fact, one story (which may or may not be true) has it that Verrocchio actually swore to give up painting when he saw Leonardo's work, since he knew he could never be that good! But even if that story were true, Verrocchio was an artist skilled in many areas, and he could just as easily have focused his talents on metalsmithing, sculpture, and bronzing. Fortunately for Verrocchio's ego, Leonardo didn't develop his skills in those areas until later!

Besides Verrocchio and Leonardo, a number of other well-known collaborators, including Sandro Botticelli and Lorenzo di Credi, were involved with the creation of *The Baptism of Christ*. Many of these artists would eventually become famous in their own rights. This masterpiece remained at the monastery in San Salvi until 1530, and it currently resides in the Uffizi Gallery in Florence.

The Company of Painters:
Membership has its privileges

With the success of *The Baptism of Christ* (see number 12), Leonardo's confidence probably hit a high point. His work was recognized far and wide, and this realization may have given him a push to leave Verrocchio's studio and strike out on his own. Though most artists based their own styles on those of their masters, Leonardo was clearly branching out and discovering his individual talents.

In 1472, Leonardo joined the Company of Painters. This group belonged to one of many guilds that existed in Italy during the Renaissance. The notion of the guild (an association, usually for either religious, craft, or business purposes) had been around since the first century, but guilds became more popular during the Middle Ages. Guilds gave artists opportunities to get together, share techniques, and provide mutual protection. They were a common resource for patrons, too.

The main types of guilds in the pre-Renaissance era were merchant and craft; merchant guilds were for businessmen, and craft guilds were for painters, architects, sculptors, and other artists. A cross between a club and a users' group, guilds provided a common interest base and promoted the development of specific trades. Generally speaking, each major city had a guild for each art. And these guilds weren't just social affairs! In some cities, guilds would design entire public-works projects.

The Company of Painters had many benefits for its members—for starters, there was the prestige and credibility. For another, guilds increased artists' visibility to potential patrons. And not anyone could just walk up and join; these artistic guilds were selective, women being perhaps the most obvious exclusion.

For Leonardo, joining the Company of Painters was a big deal. While he kept working out of his master's studio, enrollment in the guild gave him a higher status and enabled him to receive commissions both individually and as part of the guild. But the honor of belonging to a guild certainly didn't come free. The guild's record books show that Leonardo was behind on his dues at least once. In typical fashion, Leonardo rebelled from within; he came out in favor of educating artists through schools, rather than apprenticeships and guilds.

Leonardo was prolific in this early period, producing many sketches and paintings. One of the first dated works attributed to Da Vinci is a pen-and-ink landscape drawing of the Arno River Valley. This sketch, from 1473, was one of many that Leonardo created before he became famous. The Uffizi Gallery in Florence contains several of the paintings Leonardo created between 1472 and 1475; one such work is the *Annunciation*, a religious scene that combined oil and tempera on wood. The National Gallery of Art in Washington houses other Leonardo paintings, such as *Madonna and Child with Pomegranate* (1472–1476) and one of his early portraits, an oil painting on wood of Ginevra de'Benci (1474–1476). Even in these early works, you can see Leonardo's innovations and genius. Not bad for a twenty-two-year-old!

Striking out on his own

After five years with the Company of Painters, Leonardo broke free of the guild and opened his own art studio in Florence. While he still kept close ties to Verrocchio, he began establishing his own identity, splitting from Verrocchio on several major issues. For example, while Verrocchio was a master of tempera, Leonardo preferred working with oil paint. Leonardo thought that oil paints had a more natural glow, and they also increased his ability to mix colors. His apprenticeship with Andrea Verrocchio gave Leonardo both the confidence and the reputation to join the Company of Painters; the experience he gained with the guild likely spurred him to branch out further by going to work for himself. In modern-day terms, Leonardo's striking out would be equivalent to working for a large corporation, and then taking out loans to begin a start-up company.

During his first years with the guild, Leonardo was still working with Verrocchio's studio on many projects. Records indicate that he either assumed more of a financial-management role with Verrocchio's jobs, or he actually had several of his own commissions within the studio. Never one to turn down work, Leonardo may have also worked with Antonio Pollaiuolo's neighboring studio on projects.

Leonardo's work during this period includes sketches he made around 1478 of an angel, which could be based on his angel from Verrocchio's *Baptism of Christ*, done several years earlier. Many paintings of the Virgin Mary done during this period have been attributed to Leonardo as well. Of particular interest is a vibrant *Madonna and Child* from 1478 that shows incredible attention to detail and human facial expression. Leonardo's *Portrait of Ginevra de'Benci*, mentioned in the previous point, was one of his first surviving Renaissance portraitures. This oil-on-wood painting shows a woman with incredibly detailed curls in her hair and a facial expression that suggests she may have been used as practice for Leonardo's later work on the *Mona Lisa*.

The *Madonna of the Carnation*, also called the *Benois Madonna* (1478–1480), is another of Leonardo's works done during this early independent period. This oil painting again demonstrated realistic human features with a rich depth of expression, apparent especially in the Madonna's facial and hand gestures. And like many of Leonardo's other artistic endeavors, this work appears to be partially incomplete. Further, in this painting, lighting appears to be coming from both behind and in front of the window, indicating that Leonardo was experimenting with the advanced painting techniques he would later refine. The innovations in Leonardo's early works are often copied throughout his career—when he found something that worked, he refined it and then used it over and over again.

Leonardo's period of self-employment was short-lived at this point. Devoted as he may have been to his art, Leonardo still had to eat and pay the bills. He didn't yet have a full-time patron, and no one would pay him just to sit around and draw for himself. Then there was the issue of handing projects in on time—something that plagued Leonardo throughout his career. Although he had a good reputation from the start, he was also known for starting more projects than he finished, and most patrons preferred a completed work to an idea or sketch—especially when they were paying for it! As it turns out, the artist-in-residence option fit Leonardo better than individual commissions. When just one patron employed him, Leonardo had much more leeway in his work. Leonardo went on to work for many important people over the course of his life, and his art developed with each change in patronage.

The rebirth of Italy

The Italian Renaissance is a truly unique part of history—it impacted society in just about every way possible, from the culture and art of the day to the religious and intellectual atmosphere. As a bit of background, Italian city-states of the fourteenth century were very different from each other: They were ruled separately, and this often created situations where one city would have enormous influence over the surrounding areas. At the beginning of the Renaissance, the main centers of power were Florence, Milan, Venice, Naples, and the region around Rome ruled by the pope. As the Renaissance spread and produced more interaction and communication between city-states, it also provided the means to create a more united Italy, and a more unified Europe.

Pre-Renaissance city-states were economically mixed. Generally speaking, rich people lived in the cities and poorer ones lived in the country. Gradually, however, the wealth spread out. As bankers and other merchants became wealthy, classes other than nobility were coming into money for the first time.

The Early Renaissance really began in Florence. There, some of the wealthiest members of society started supporting humanities and the arts. Writing, painting, sculpture, architecture, and science were all fields that were suddenly in the public eye. The Medicis were one of the most influential families during the Renaissance and would turn out to be one of Leonardo's many patrons. Lorenzo de Medici (1449–1492), son of Cosimo de Medici (one of the period's wealthiest Italians), gained popular acknowledgement and support by funding art and architecture.

In spite of newfound money and culture, life was not entirely peaceful during the Renaissance. In 1454, Milan, Florence, and Naples were united under the Treaty of Lodi, through which each city attempted to ally itself with the others. But thanks to Pope Alexander VI's scheming goals, the French King Charles VIII headed up an Italian invasion and several areas were conquered as a result.

Then, in 1495, King Ferdinand of Spain got involved and helped to create the League of Venice, which included Spain and other Italian city-states. France invaded Italy on several other occasions during this period, contributing to the political unrest so characteristic of the Renaissance. The popes of this era (Alexander VI, Julius II, and Leo X) served mainly to enforce a Christian system of beliefs throughout the country, in part by preventing Ottoman invasion. By 1527, the Holy Roman Empire had taken over what was left of the city- and papal-states.

But enough about the attacks on Italy during the Renaissance; let's get back to the great cultural strides made during this period. Humanism was the Renaissance's most important conceptual innovation. This idea of a human-based study included a revival of classical beliefs from ancient Greece and Rome.

The hallmark characteristics of the Renaissance peaked between about 1490 and 1527, when German and Spanish imperial troops sacked Rome. This period, when Leonardo da Vinci did much of his work, is usually called the High Renaissance because it represents a culmination of all the ideas that had been floating around Florence in the previous years. The main idea was that beauty could be achieved by combining classical forms with landscapes, cityscapes, and other "natural" elements. Unlike the Early Renaissance (which centered mostly around Florence), other parts of Italy, including Rome and Milan, felt the High Renaissance's influence.

In addition to Leonardo da Vinci, other famous artists of the High Renaissance include Michelangelo Buonarroti (1475–1564) and Raphael (1483–1520). Like Leonardo, Michelangelo and Raphael both studied in Florence and worked in painting, architecture, and other arts.

Renaissance religion

The Renaissance had the biggest impact on the humanities, arts, and sciences. As with everything in Europe at that time, however, there were also religious implications. Papal states (regions run by the pope, who served as the bishop of Rome) were as important politically as the city-states, which included Florence and Milan.

At the beginning of the High Renaissance, Pope Julius II (reigning 1503–1513) was in power. Though a religious figure, religion wasn't the only thing he influenced! Julius II's goals were also politically and geographically motivated. He strove to remove the French from Italian territory before they could completely take over the Italian papacy. By 1512 Italy had joined Spain in the Holy League and the countries united to defeat the French, thus scoring a victory for both Christianity and Italy.

During this period, popes were often expelled for bribery or other treacheries, but their power was usually restored. To this extent, religious leadership was consistent but not absolute. Popes also often handed their office over to close friends and family members, and this culture of nepotism contributed to the unrest. Further, popes led privileged lives and had access to luxuries that much of the population would never experience. Consequently, although they were respected and feared for their connections to God, people looked at them with suspicion. High-level politicians would even marry off their daughters to popes or papal families. Lorenzo de Medici, for example, had his daughter Magdalena marry a pope's son. Not a bad way to ensure a solid connection between religion and government!

A fragile stability was reached during the early sixteenth century, and by the middle of the sixteenth century, virtually all of Italy was at least nominally Roman Catholic. The Roman Catholic Church's corruptions were apparent, however. The close union of religion with politics and wealth dismantled the very nature of the Church as an institution of holiness. People were also dissatisfied with the emphasis the Church placed on ritual, rather than personal prayer. Then, in 1517, Martin Luther (1483–1546) unknowingly sparked the Protestant Reformation when he nailed his Ninety-five Theses to the door of the Castle Church in Wittenberg, Germany (see number 82). The Protestant

Reformation attempted to transform the Church by calling for a return to the Bible's teachings. Since religious revolution was a popular idea at the time, people from all over Europe joined in support. Because of the Reformation, the Church was ultimately forced to revise its close dependency on outside groups. But the Reformation also caused a split in the Catholic Church, as new Protestant groups such as Lutherans and Anabaptists were created.

It's amazing to think that Leonardo and other Renaissance artists were creating their masterpieces amid all this political turmoil and religious unrest. Even though the Church was still entrenched in its strongholds from the Middle Ages, the Renaissance helped artists to break from tradition and, in many ways, address their art in a more personal fashion. The Protestant Reformation gained strength as Leonardo neared the end of his life, but the general feeling of social unrest remained prevalent throughout his most productive years.

Don't forget the golden oldies

While the Renaissance celebrated humanism and individual abilities, it was also an era that remembered the past. Classical Greek and Roman antiquity was reborn during the Renaissance. People believed that the ancient Greeks and Romans had gotten things right: Their art had rules—and good rules at that. The certainty of the classics provided a calming effect that Leonardo and his contemporaries were desperate to incorporate during such troubled times.

One of the most attractive elements of this classical revival was a sense of beauty and proportion. Classical architecture used balance and harmony for its aesthetic appeal and symbolically religious nature. Inner and outer beauty were equivalent in classical sculptures. Greek statues were notoriously well proportioned, a balance that was created in order to please the gods and, by association, the surrounding world.

The idea of balance extended to architecture as well. Classical temples with ordered plans and symmetrical columns produced a sense of order that Renaissance architects tried to recapture. Three major Greek orders, or architectural styles, emerged, providing a clean way to organize form and structure. The three orders, Doric, Ionic, and Corinthian, are best known for the columns with those names. Because classical temples were completely devoted to the gods for whom they were named, their proportions had to be symbolic of the gods' perfection. The idea was that an ordered space should project that order onto its inhabitants, sort of like a clean desk inspiring you to work more efficiently.

There was a bit of nostalgia at work here, too. When it came to looking back to the antiquities, Renaissance artists adopted the familiar "grass is always greener on the other side" philosophy. In their view, Greek and Roman culture provided strong role models, little apparent corruption (at least compared to what Renaissance artists faced), and some vague notion of a glorious past. These were strong ideals, and Leonardo and his contemporaries embraced them eagerly. The Renaissance Church was, of course, still a powerful influence in the lives of fifteenth- and sixteenth-century Italians, and maybe its strong presence stood in stark contrast to the perceived serenity and order of their Greek and Roman predecessors.

Reading and writing in classical languages such as Latin was popular during the Renaissance. Although Leonardo probably wasn't able to study original Latin texts, many of his works do show a careful study of classicism. For instance, his *Adoration of the Magi* has architectural elements in the background that show a distinctly classical influence. Similarly, *Annunciation* uses Greek-like cornerstones, as well as other architectural elements, which likely came from Leonardo's interest in the classics. He did, though, add a Renaissance twist by giving the stones rough surfaces and pronounced joints instead of a smooth, classical-era finish. How typical of Leonardo to take an established style and make it his own! Another of Leonardo's major works, *The Last Supper*, uses a careful sense of proportion and symmetry to reflect a divine influence—certainly appropriate for the subject matter. This idea was actually derived directly from Greek and Roman design and construction methods.

Show me the money!

The start of the Italian Renaissance also meant the restoration of trade, which had almost completely dried up during the Middle Ages. As populations grew and prosperous city-states expanded in Italy, England, and France, trade increased as well. The first order of business was shipping luxury goods from the Mediterranean to Italian port cities such as Pisa, Genoa, and Venice. Situated between Western Europe and the Mediterranean, Italy was in a great location to become a major trade center. These port cities got bigger and wealthier as trade increased, which, in turn, caused changes in many aspects of society, including art and finance.

As trade increased the flow of money through Italy's port cities and those with secondary industries such as banking started to flourish. Florence, Leonardo da Vinci's home region, became Italy's central banking city in the early fourteenth century, which included the bank of the influential Medici family. Although based in Florence, the Medici's bank had branches in other cities across Italy and the rest of Europe. The bank financed a variety of projects, and its substantial profits were invested in the political and cultural life of Florence and other Italian cities.

As commerce grew, people in the trading and banking industries came to towns to interact and profit. Trade opened up the world beyond the confines of traditional town walls, and openness to new ideas and innovations spread to other parts of society. Towns and cities grew, and peasants migrating to towns from the countryside helped to create a new class structure. These former country folks became the working class, whereas the noble people and wealthy merchants became the ruling class. These urban elite led the Renaissance's political and cultural changes, while the rural poor participated very little.

The closing of trade routes to China during the Italian Renaissance also had a big economic influence. Beginning with thirteenth-century Venetian explorer Marco Polo and his famous trip to China, Italy established complicated routes to China and the Far East to trade luxuries like spices and silk. However, when the Ming Dynasty came to power in the fourteenth century, China closed trade with outsiders. Suddenly, the wealth and resources that would have previously gone into foreign trade were instead available for projects within Italy. The rich ruling merchant class began to invest in Italian society, commissioning myriad works of art and architecture that enriched the culture. Individual artists who received these commissions, like Leonardo, also benefited from this process.

Another innovation, the printing press, had a large effect on the spread of knowledge during the Renaissance. In 1452, the printing of Johannes Gutenberg's famous Gutenberg Bible served as an early example of movable type's possibilities (see number 61). While Germany took the early lead in printing efforts, Italy soon took up the challenge, establishing presses that printed affordable copies of classical texts and other works. Suddenly, knowledge was easier to spread—libraries could serve as repositories for information, and people could afford to buy printed books instead of expensive hand-copied volumes. Leonardo da Vinci, among many others, gleaned much knowledge in his early years from the volumes of books available in his family and friends' libraries. And he definitely put this knowledge to good use.

The importance of being sponsored

Everyone knows about the stereotype of the starving artist. Even during the Renaissance, when artists were important members of society, patronage was one of the only ways an artist could earn a living while devoting himself to— you guessed it—making art. While some Renaissance artists had to find other work to pay the bills, many searched high and low for a patron—someone to sponsor their artistic development. And having a patron was much better than the Renaissance equivalent of waiting tables!

The idea of having the Church or other groups sponsor artists and particular artworks began well before the Renaissance. In Medieval times the Church sponsored many religious works of art, and during the Middle Ages there were groups of secular politicians (kings, noblemen, and princes) who would come together in sponsoring artists to create both religious and secular works.

The Renaissance took patronage to a new level. In some cases, a wealthy individual would bring an artist into his home, providing food and shelter in exchange for art. Alternatively, a person or group would commission a particular work of art, and the artist would be employed until the work's completion.

Depending on the size and scope, these commissioned works could take years to finish. In that respect, these two types of patronage were sometimes nearly equivalent, although commissioned artwork gave the artist more independence than the artist-in-residence option.

Religion was one of the most significant reasons for art's popularity during this time. Sponsoring a religious work of art made you appear more pious, putting you in good stead with the Church and conferring greater prestige on your family. Wealthy families lived in the public eye; to be perceived as wealthy, people had to surround themselves with beauty—particularly beauty created expressly for them. The ability to afford commissioned artwork was a sign of power, and Renaissance politicians and other leading figures were not shy about flaunting their wealth. Leonardo appeared, for a time, to be happy to oblige the wealthy in this endeavor. And who can blame him? If nothing else, it probably paid well.

Patronage was also a matter of simple aesthetics. In a world before television, movies, and popular culture, appreciating fine sculpture or painting was a pleasure for many people. Those who could afford art created by the masters chose to support it, and in return, they were able to surround themselves with the most incredible and skilled art of the period.

In addition to wealthy individuals (including kings and political figures), collective patronage was also popular during the Renaissance. For example, the wool guild patronized artwork in the Florence Cathedral and sponsored a competition for the design of the baptistery doors. Not too different from corporate sponsorships of cultural events today!

The relationship between patron and artist was usually quite formal. Most of the time a contract was involved, requiring the artist to create a specified number of pieces. Some patrons, particularly ones with a lot of cash to throw around, sponsored artists to work more or less at their whim. If this arrangement worked, then everyone was happy; if the obligations of the contract weren't met, however, patronage could be terminated and the artist would be dismissed. Many different patrons sponsored Leonardo over the course of his life. While in most cases he was likely terminated for reasons beyond his control, it's also possible that Leonardo ended some of the relationships on his own.

Generally, when artist and patron argued, it was over money—as in the artist wanted a raise but the patron didn't want to shell out. In Leonardo da Vinci's case, there were lots of arguments over his inability to complete projects. You can't blame the patrons for wanting what they paid for. In some cases, the style or content of a particular work sparked disagreements. Early in the Renaissance, patrons more or less had complete control over their artists. As the Renaissance progressed and art became more highly valued, however, artists demanded more freedom when it came to their work.

Lorenzo the Magnificent

Want a way to enhance your political reputation? Today's politicians might support a worthy cause, but it was different during the Renaissance. Back then sponsoring an artist was all the rage. Some patrons would actually specify the quantity of gold, silver, and other precious metals they wanted artists to include in their paintings! These measurements assured patrons of bragging rights for having the most expensive sculpture or the most precious painting.

In Renaissance Florence, the Medicis were the most important political family (see number 15). The richest family in Italy (and perhaps in Europe), they spent a great deal of money building churches, supporting art, giving to charity, and constructing family monuments to ensure their continued political and social control. They were like Renaissance Vanderbilts or Rockefellers. During Leonardo's time, Lorenzo de' Medici (also known as Lorenzo the Magnificent) ruled Florence. Thanks to Lorenzo's avid support of the arts, Florence rose to a central position in the Renaissance artistic world. As the cultural center of Europe, Florence also became the founding location of the new humanist movement. Florence was certainly the place to be!

Under the Medici family, patronage grew to include more than just single works of art. The Medicis commissioned not only gardens, fountains, and public sculptures, but also residences, government centers, fortified compounds, artistic institutions, and even intricately staged public events. Was there anything they didn't commission? When you're the richest family in Europe, you get what you want.

By 1480, Leonardo had established his own studio in Florence and became well known enough to acquire a patron. He became a member of the garden of San Marcos, which was under Lorenzo de' Medici's patronage. (Lorenzo was Michelangelo's patron as well.)

During this time, Leonardo was commissioned to paint *Adoration of the Magi* for the monastery altar of San Donato Scopeto. The scene shows the Three Kings along with Mary and her infant son. Although Leonardo was given more than two years to work on this piece, even that wasn't enough time. He managed to finish enough of it to show that he was well on his way to breaking away from Verrocchio's influence. The style is different from his previous works, with a triangular grouping of people in the foreground and an elaborate background that combines natural and architectural elements. While many works of the day were composed linearly, a straight line was just too boring for Leonardo. *Adoration* has a balanced, symmetrical structure, again showcasing Leonardo's rapidly developing independence.

While under Lorenzo de' Medici's patronage, Leonardo worked on other paintings such as *San Gerolamo*. Unfortunately, this patron-artist arrangement did not last for long. Leonardo was a strong-spirited artist with a reputation for not finishing everything he started, and Lorenzo the Magnificent expected his sponsored works to be completed. With a name like Magnificent, you expect things to be done your way! After a few years, it was time for Leonardo to move on.

21

Playing up to the duke

In 1482, Leonardo applied for patronage with the soon to be Duke of Milan, Ludovico Sforza. Like the Medici family in Florence, the Sforzas controlled Milan at this time. However, unlike the banking Medicis, the Sforzas were warriors. Some members of the Sforza family were actually *condottierei*, mercenary soldiers who fought in wars for the highest bidder. The Sforzas rose through the military classes over time, eventually gaining control over Milan from about 1450 to 1535. Just imagine the young Leonardo trying to find his place working for them.

Ludovico became duke in 1494. Although he initially aligned himself with the French King Charles, he later fought against France in an attempt to protect Milan. Duke Sforza was certainly quite a warrior, at one point making weapons from up to seventy tons of bronze that had previously been earmarked for one of Leonardo's sculptures (see number 29). Leonardo couldn't have been too pleased about that turn of events.

Leonardo likely learned about military equipment and machinery during his tenure under the duke. He became Ludovico's court painter, a relationship that lasted until 1499. In that year, Sforza's land was invaded and he was forcibly driven out of Milan. The French King Louis XII invoked a claim on Sforza's property, and Ludovico ultimately died in a French prison. So much for the great warrior, and for Leonardo's great patron.

While Sforza spent a lot of time embroiled in political turmoil, he made a point of investing in the arts and especially in Leonardo da Vinci. Under Sforza's patronage, Leonardo created some of his most famous works. When applying for the job with Sforza, Leonardo wrote a detailed list of his engineering and military credentials, with his artistic skills listed almost as an afterthought. Fortunately, Sforza took advantage of all of Leonardo's talents!

Leonardo came into his own while under the Duke of Milan's patronage. He got the chance to experiment with painting, sculpture, weapons design, architecture, and machinery. Leonardo was an artist, but he was also a realist; he understood the necessity of defense, even though he didn't agree with the concept of war. Of course, he also didn't want to alienate his sponsor. As the duke's chief military engineer, Leonardo invented several different war machines and weapons during this period.

Beyond his military inventions, Leonardo created two of his most famous paintings while in Milan. He started *The Virgin of the Rocks* in 1483, a painting intended for the altar at the Chapel of the Immacolata, located in the church of San Francesco Grande. The contract was extremely specific: The monks wanted the painting to be composed in a certain way, and it had to be done using certain materials. As you'll see in number 36, the notoriously individualistic Leonardo quickly ran into problems.

During this period, Leonardo also began work on *The Last Supper* (see number 37). Commissioned by the Duke of Milan himself, this work was to be painted on the refectory wall of the family chapel, the church of Santa Maria delle Grazie in Milan. The giant mural was almost thirty feet long—pretty amazing that it was actually completed. However, it began to deteriorate almost immediately, most likely due to the type of paints Leonardo used and the extreme humidity of the refectory's walls. Many attempts were made to restore it over time, culminating with a painstaking effort finished in 1999.

22

Look out, it's Cesare Borgia!

One of the Renaissance's more notorious political figures, Cesare Borgia (the Duke of Valencia) lived from 1476 to 1507. Born out of wedlock, he was actually the son of Pope Alexander VI. Initially, Borgia set out on the path to become a cleric, but he wound up as the Archbishop of Valencia (modern-day Spain) while his father was traveling down the road to papacy. Supposedly one of his father's favorites, Borgia probably used his family connections to obtain several official positions.

You may recognize the name Cesare Borgia as the murdering Renaissance politico who killed his own brother. Rumor has it that he did indeed murder his sibling, Giovanni, in 1497. There isn't much proof, although Cesare was said to have been jealous of his brother's high social position, and may have also fought with him over a woman. He had a violent reputation and may have been responsible for several other murders. Sounds like an all-around nice guy, right?

In 1498, Borgia did an about-face, changing his unruly ways after assuming the role of general of the Church. Because he was the illegitimate son of a priest, he had a hard time finding a suitable royal bride, so he spent much of the following year traveling, promoting his career, and dealing with various responsibilities. He also led the efforts to unite the fighting Italian city-states.

By the early 1500s, Borgia owned land all over Italy, at least part of which he had taken by force. He was quite a character—in between the murdering and the stealing, somehow he found time to be crowned Duke of Romagna for a period! As his power grew, so did his enemies. When his father died in 1503, Cesare was forced to leave Rome. It all went downhill from there. His power slowly waned, his lands were overtaken, and his castles fell into his enemies' hands. Borgia was imprisoned on several occasions and, in a fitting end to a life of crime, he was killed while attempting to take over a castle in 1507.

Needless to say, Cesare Borgia's infamy guaranteed him a place in history. Renaissance writer and philosopher Niccolo' Machiavelli (1469–1527) may even have based *The Prince*, his political examination of the day's monarchy, on Borgia's life. It is also possible that Machiavelli's work was more parody than praise; in any event, Borgia's contemporary influence was enormous and undeniable.

So how did this ruthless character relate to Renaissance master painter Leonardo da Vinci? For starters, Leonardo traveled with Cesare Borgia in the early 1500s. As a military engineer and architect, Leonardo was put to work designing war machines. When his former patron, Duke Sforza, was driven out of Rome, Leonardo had to look for work, and the military experience Leonardo gained while working under the duke helped him to secure the position with Borgia's army. During his time with Borgia, Leonardo designed many machines, including collapsible bridges, wall-mounted ladders, and rotating scythe blades attached to moving chariots. It's also possible that he designed weapons, such as catapults, crossbows, machine guns, and cannons. Leonardo's genius turned lethal, when required.

Like so many religious and political figures of the day, Borgia was also a patron of the arts, and having Leonardo da Vinci in his company was another feather in his cap. Leonardo stayed with Cesare Borgia until his return to Milan in 1506.

The best of the Louis

King Louis XII of France (1462–1515), affectionately dubbed "Father of the People," was a popular king who had a major influence during the Renaissance. In a typically nepotistic fashion, he inherited a duke position from his father, the Duke of Orleans. Like Leonardo, he stood up for what he believed in as part of the rebellion against the French King Charles (who was, incidentally, his cousin). This little incident landed him in prison from 1487 to 1490, but later, he worked his way back into Charles's circle of friends. How forgiving!

But how'd he end up in Italy? At that time, many powerful French leaders were asserting their claims to dominance in Italy. Louis was part of this movement, and he made a name for himself by participating in the Italian invasions. He went on to become king upon Charles's death in 1498.

After gaining power over Milan in 1500, Louis had the unenviable task of dividing the royal authority in Naples and engaging in constant battles for power with Spain. He also had to suppress the Italian city-states' various rebellions, including those in Genoa and Venice. Around 1511, however, Pope Julius II formed the Holy Roman League, one of its main purposes being to eradicate French leadership in Italy. Louis remained in power in Milan until 1513, when the French presence was driven out. In 1514, King Louis's second wife died, and he remarried Mary Tudor, King Henry VIII's eighteen-year-old sister. When Louis XII died in 1515, the French monarchy went to François I.

As king, Louis was popular among the people because he lowered taxes and made other general improvements. He was also a patron of the arts, and Leonardo da Vinci served as his court painter in Milan for several years.

After his stint as Cesare Borgia's military engineer, Leonardo returned to Milan. He was becoming increasingly famous, and King Louis's governor, Charles D'Amboise, requested him specifically for the position of court painter. Leonardo's reputation was well established by this time, and King Louis's court wanted to get in on the national treasure that Leonardo was becoming. You can tell that Leonardo was in high demand from a letter King Louis's court sent to the city of Florence, asking for Leonardo's services. Hard to imagine the Queen of England writing to the entire City of New York to ask for a painter, isn't it? King Louis wanted Leonardo to remain in Milan until his highness could set up court there, and of course Leonardo obliged.

In addition to painting, Leonardo provided architectural, military, and other engineering services to King Louis. He was also responsible for other general duties as directed by the court; when Louis traveled to other cities, Leonardo may have been in charge of decorations and whatever traveling road show the king required. All in all, it was a very sweet deal for our master painter.

Leonardo painted several masterpieces during this period. In 1506, he worked on a second version of *The Virgin of the Rocks*. He also painted *Leda and the Swan* (now lost) and *The Virgin and Saint Anne* in 1509, as well as *St. John in the Wilderness* from around 1510 to 1515.

Leonardo also took this opportunity to do some prefunded, independent study. He was fascinated with botany, hydraulics, mechanics, and other sciences. He took his study of anatomy to a higher level, and in working with the noted anatomist Marcantonio della Torre from the University of Pavia, he learned much, storing his knowledge away for future use in paintings, writings, and other designs. But Leonardo did more than just study. In 1512, he produced one of his first self-portraits. Then, of course, there were the legal distractions related to settling his father's and uncle's estates (see number 5).

Leonardo remained Louis XII's court painter until the king was forced out of Milan in 1513. At this time, Leonardo left Milan briefly and found work in Florence and Rome over the next several years.

Don't mess with the pope

One of the most important political, social, and religious units in Florence, the Medici family controlled the republic more than the government possibly could have. While the family was historically composed of doctors and artists, they later became bankers and ran the region financially.

In the early sixteenth century Giovanni de Medici, son of Lorenzo the Magnificent, rose to be a cardinal in the Roman Catholic Church. But the Medicis certainly weren't the only powerful family in Italy. Other families challenged their financial and cultural control, but Giovanni used his connections with the pope to reassert the Medicis as a primary ruling family. Ultimately, Giovanni became Pope Leo X. His greatest claim to fame, incidentally, is being the pope who was responsible for Martin Luther's excommunication during the Protestant Reformation.

Giovanni's brother, Giuliano de' Medici, was also a great success as head of the pope's army. Art historians in particular like to study Giuliano because he served as Leonardo da Vinci's patron from 1513–1516. After King Louis XII of France was forced out of power in Milan in 1513, Leonardo was freed from his role as court painter and quickly got back on good terms with the Medici family.

Leonardo da Vinci's lifestyle underwent major changes during these years. He moved to Rome and lived in the Vatican, where he earned respect from both religious authorities and other artists. Respect equaled more commissions, so he was making friends in the right places. He had his own workshop in Rome and took on many projects under the direction of both Giuliano de Medici and the pope.

Having such a high position gave Leonardo luxuries that other artists didn't have; he had free time to study, and he focused his efforts on learning more about anatomy and physiology. During the course of his studies, Leonardo became convinced of the scientific importance of dissecting human cadavers. This approach certainly made sense, given what Renaissance doctors and scientists were beginning to understand about the human body. However, much to Leonardo's dismay, the pope issued orders expressly forbidding the dissection of human bodies. Faced with no other choice, Leonardo reluctantly obeyed.

While in Rome, Leonardo was in close proximity to some of his primary rivals. Both Michelangelo and Raphael were becoming major players in the art world, and while Leonardo didn't have much direct contact with these artists, their obvious abilities certainly prodded him to keep up, if not surpass them.

Da Vinci created several masterpieces while under Giuliano de Medici's patronage. One of his crowning achievements was *St. John the Baptist* (1513–1516), which may be the last painting Leonardo ever worked on. This painting is particularly significant because it clearly demonstrates *sfumato*, a technique Leonardo developed over the course of his career to make people and objects appear to dissolve into one other and the accompanying background (see number 30). You can see another excellent example of *sfumato* in Leonardo's *Mona Lisa* (1503–1506).

Among Leonardo's later technical achievements during his period in Rome was a mechanical lion he developed for the coronation of France's successor to the crown, King François I. Following the coronation in 1516, Leonardo again joined the royal courts, serving under François, until his death in 1519.

25

François I, King of France and friend of Leonardo

After his years of travel with Cesare Borgia and his army, Leonardo probably needed a break. He was, after all, in his fifties at the turn of the century, and the nomadic warrior lifestyle wasn't exactly restful. As explained in the previous points, Leonardo's occupations after moving to Milan were varied: he worked as court painter, engineer, architect, and all-around artist for Louis XII between 1506 and 1513. Then, the Medicis were his patrons in Rome until 1516.

From 1516 to until his death in 1519, Leonardo worked for the court of François I (1494–1547), the King of France. François was crowned in 1515 after he inherited the monarchy from Louis XII. Often considered to be the first true king of the Renaissance, François was enchanted with the artwork of the day, and he reportedly invited Leonardo to visit the French court and ultimately convinced him to stay. Once there, Leonardo was honored and respected, as well he should have been! Rather than being simply a court painter, he was given the title of Premier Architect, Engineer, and Painter.

While some of his earlier accommodations were little more than stable rooms, Da Vinci's final home was a luxurious house near the royal palace in France. He lived at the Clos Luce Manor, located in the Loire Valley. And the free room and board wasn't all—Leonardo was well paid for his work during these final years and was reputed to have been closer to François than any of his previous patrons. Apparently, the king did not ask Leonardo to produce much toward the end of his life. His primary role was to serve as the king's friend. There may have even been an underground passage between the Manor and royal castle, which would have given the king easy access to his aging friend.

Toward the end of his life, Leonardo spent much time sketching. He developed some of the first sketches of water flowing freely and circulating in a whirlpool. Later, scientists researching turbulence would actually study his drawings. Leonardo also developed preliminary designs for scuba gear, diving suits, movable bridges, underwater craft, and many other devices that foretold designs to come.

François, by all accounts, had a special place in his heart for Leonardo and the feeling appears to have been mutual. Leonardo's favorite work was the *Mona Lisa*, which he kept with him at all times, until, as evidence suggests, he either gave or sold his treasure to King François.

King François remained a patron of the arts after Leonardo's death; he collected masterpieces from other artists, including Michelangelo, Cellini, Raphael, and Titian. His royal palace, decorated with works from Leonardo and others, was a true tribute to Renaissance art. What an amazing museum it would have made.

Da Vinci University

Wish you could have signed up for painting classes with the Great Leonardo? Even if you were alive during the Renaissance, you would have had a tough time. Leonardo never established a formal school or workshop. However, he did instruct plenty of students and apprentices over the years. During Leonardo's years in Milan at the court of Sforza, he probably had a number of apprentices and pupils. He even wrote training guides specifically for these students, and these documents were later collected in book form as *A Treatise on Painting*.

Leonardo was a hands-on teacher and also collaborated on a number of works with his students during this period, some of which still have questionable attributions. Several of his students' works have even been incorrectly attributed to Leonardo himself. This collaborative style makes it hard to place blame for mistakes, and also makes it hard to give credit where credit is due.

Da Vinci's pupils during this Milan period included Giovanni Antonio Boltraffio (his earliest pupil); Bernardino de'Conti; Giacomo Caprotti (nicknamed Salai); Giovanni Agostino da Lodi; Andrea Solario; Ambrogio de Predis; Francesco Napoletano; and Marco d'Oggiono. While Leonardo was in Milan in the early 1500s, Bernadino de'Conti and Salai continued as his apprentices. He also had a new crop of assistants, including Bernardino Luini, Cesare de Sesto, Giampetrino, and Francesco Melzi. (Melzi later became his personal companion, artistic heir, and likely lover.) Some of these pupils eventually succeeded in their own right, painting famous works such as *La Belle Ferronniere*, *Lucrezia Crivelli*, and the *Madonna Litta*.

Leonardo reportedly chose some of his assistants for their good looks rather than their artistic abilities (Francesco Melzi and Salai in particular). Melzi, unlike Salai, did produce a few paintings during his many years with Leonardo, so we know that the relationship was at least slightly more than personal!

The commission to paint *The Virgin of the Rocks*, one of the master's early major works, was actually given to both Leonardo and his assistant, Ambrogio de Predis, in 1483. Ambrogio served as a court painter to Ludovico Sforza and hosted Leonardo in his home when Leonardo first came to Milan. The two collaborated on paintings throughout the 1490s, and *The Virgin of the Rocks* is the best known of these collaborations. In this work, Leonardo painted the central picture, while de Predis painted two side panels showing angels playing musical instruments. Two versions were eventually completed, thanks to the resulting lawsuit (see number 36 for the complete story on this work). Although in the later version the angel kneeling behind the infant Jesus is undoubtedly Leonardo's work, he most likely did not finish it. The Madonna and landscape aren't as good technically, suggesting that a student probably painted them.

One of Leonardo's students from Milan, Andrea Solario (1460–1524), made his own style by mixing elements of Leonardo's work with the contemporary Lombard and Venetian schools of painting. His bright colors, fantastical landscapes, and harmonious groupings of figures emulate Leonardo, while some of his naturalistic details echo the Lombard and Flemish traditions. Leonardo probably used another one of his Milan students, Boltraffio, as a test bed for his teaching, and it seems to have paid off. Boltraffio's training is visible in many of his works, including his 1495 painting *The Virgin and the Child*, which he may have based on Leonardo's sketches.

Later in Leonardo's life, during his final years in Rome (around 1509–1516), he continued to have many students. In fact, Leonardo's students copied his final painting, *St. John the Baptist*, many times. Since many of Leonardo's original works are now lost, in many cases, only copies done by his pupils allow us to see the true scope of his work. Though Leonardo's students spent much time copying the master's works, few of them ever transcended his direct influence to become well known in their own right. Only two of Leonardo's followers, Bernardino Luini and Sodoma, seem to have developed well-respected careers independent of Leonardo.

Bernardino Luini, a Milanese painter, was born sometime between 1470 and 1480, and lived until 1530. It's assumed that he was Leonardo's student, though there's no actual evidence to support that claim. A number of Luini's works, including *Christ Crowned with Thorns* and some of his paintings of the Virgin and Child (such as those at Saronno) show a style similar to Leonardo's in terms of color choices, overall design, and the sense of depth given by the paintings' relief elements. In these aspects, Luini came closer to replicating Leonardo's style than any other contemporary artist.

But Luini's style was, in many ways, distinctly his own. For one thing, his works have a sweetness that Leonardo's more ambiguous paintings lack. Also, Luini's works are generally more religious than Leonardo's. Many of Luini's frescos are well known, and while Luini certainly was not a master of many fields as was Leonardo, his works do an admirable job of instilling a sense of religious stillness in observers.

Giovanni Antonio Bazzi (1477–1549) is another artist whom Leonardo influenced significantly, although once again, there is no evidence that he studied directly in Leonardo's studio. Known by his nickname, Sodoma, Bazzi came to Milan in the late 1400s as a glass painter's apprentice. Sodoma was a natural at drawing, but he learned several things from Leonardo, including color selection. His works are often charming and poetic, and the faces of the women and children he created are quite beautiful. However, none of his works have the timeless mystery and appeal of Leonardo's, showing that once again, genius is a hard act to follow!

Part 2

THE BEST OF THE BEST OF THE BEST

Though Leonardo's interests were all over the map, today we primarily know him for his paintings, and for good reason. They demonstrate Leonardo's various technical innovations, including the blending techniques of *sfumato* and *chiaroscuro*. Leonardo pioneered the use of realistic perspectives in his paintings, and he brought his scenes to life with fantastical backgrounds. The *Mona Lisa* is probably his most famous painting today, but some of his lesser-known works were also immensely popular during his lifetime.

So what could he do besides paint, you ask? Plenty—Leonardo was a talented innovator in many other artistic fields. He produced designs for sculptures, including what would have been the largest bronze sculpture ever cast if it had been built. With his background in both art and mathematics, Leonardo was a natural for architecture—he designed a number of churches, palaces, fortresses, and military structures. He also devoted time to a personal project called "Ideal City," a master plan for city planning meant to provide a hygienic urban design to protect city dwellers from the plagues that decimated populations during Leonardo's lifetime. While none of Leonardo's architectural designs were ever built, other contemporary architects did adopt some of his concepts.

Whether painting his most famous works, like the *Mona Lisa* and *The Last Supper*, or planning new and innovative city structures, Leonardo's expertise and breadth of knowledge reached far beyond traditional areas of art and architecture.

27

Early sculpture:
A celebration in three dimensions

During his apprenticeship to Andrea Verrocchio (1468–1472), Leonardo learned how to paint—but his education didn't stop there. He was exposed to different aspects of arts and craftsmanship, including how to make panels and canvases, castings, and sculptures. Leonardo was a bit biased in that he considered painting to be the true sign of genius in an artist. Leonardo viewed sculpture as being more mechanical, whereas he saw painting as more expressive and creative. Lucky for us he excelled at both.

Leonardo's early experiments with sculpture focused on the human emotions. During this period, he created several busts of women demonstrating various expressions, including smiles and laughter. His interest in mathematics probably enhanced his ability to create geometrically precise sculptures and busts.

Many Renaissance sculptors took inspiration from the classics. Michelangelo and Raphael, for example, studied classical proportions, styles, and technique. You can see classical motifs in much of their work. Leonardo, on the other hand, was more of an individualist. You can see his personal style in all of his work, particularly in his approach to three-dimensional art.

Sculpture, for Leonardo, wasn't just about the final result. He also used sculptures to enhance his paintings. Leonardo made clay studies of things like draperies, which he then used as models for his paintings. He most likely used this technique primarily in his early works, such as the draperies on the angel he painted as part of Verrocchio's *Baptism of Christ*.

Bust of a Woman with Flowers is supposedly one of Leonardo's first marble sculptures. But did Leonardo really create it? Historians know that this sculpture was made sometime between 1470 and 1480, placing it squarely within the years that Leonardo worked with Verrocchio. Stylistically, it resembles Leonardo's work more than his master's; while this sculpture was originally credited to Verrocchio, experts now think Leonardo was its primary sculptor.

This particular bust was probably created from a live model, Ginevra de'Benci, also a model for one of Leonardo's early paintings in 1474. De'Benci, who came from an educated family of bankers, was one of the most famous female intellectuals and poets of her day. This work is particularly significant because, unlike classical busts that typically only show the figure's head and shoulders, this one displays the figure's hands and arms as well. Just as Renaissance portrait paintings were starting to show people in three-quarter (rather than frontal) view, sculptures were also beginning to show more and more of the whole person. This transition relates back to the Renaissance focus on humanism. As society began to place more emphasis on the individual and his or her personal dignity, artists such as Leonardo embraced this new social movement by allowing more individual expression in artwork.

Form, function, and the whole nine yards

It's difficult to know which works are actually Leonardo's because he belonged to Verrocchio's workshop for years, and then had his own students afterwards. One of the few pieces about which there is no doubt, though, is a bronze statue called *Horse and Rider*. It dates with relative certainty to Leonardo's late years, 1516–1519. During this period, he made several models of horses for the King of France, François I.

This particular statue, featuring a horse rearing up on its hind legs, looks a lot like other horse-and-rider sculptures Leonardo made earlier in his career. The biggest of them all was the colossal *Statue of Francesco Sforza* (see number 29), a full-size monument designed in the 1480s, which was never completed in its planned form.

Leonardo was also involved with a horse-and-rider sculpture created for the funeral monument of Gian Giacomo Trivulzio. From the sketches, we can tell that this sculpture would have been quite a spectacle, having a marble base and eight other figures. The horse would have followed the same basic design as the aforementioned Sforza monument, only with a more dynamic posture. There is no evidence, however, that the work was ever completed.

If, at this point, it's beginning to seem as if Leonardo rarely completed *any* of the sculptures he concocted, this isn't the case. It's nearly certain that Leonardo sculpted other pieces that were indeed finished, such as *The Young Christ*.

Leonardo worked on this terracotta statue between 1470 and 1480, roughly the same period during which historians believe he created *Bust of a Woman with Flowers*.

In addition to these accomplishments, Leonardo worked on sculptures executed mainly by others in his workshop, such as *St. John the Baptist Teaching*, a bronze completed in 1511. Giovanni Francesco Rustici, a student originally in the Medici Garden, sculpted this statue in large part. Leonardo and Rustici met in Verrocchio's workshop, and Rustici worked alongside Leonardo for many years afterwards. Rustici could have been famous by way of patronage to popes and kings but, unlike Leonardo, he didn't seem to have much ambition and preferred to be alone. Fortunately, since he came from a wealthy family, he had the luxury of doing as he wished.

In the early 1500s, Rustici was working with a local merchants' guild commissioned to create bronze statues for the church of San Giovanni. The star attraction was to be a sculpture of St. John the Baptist. As the story goes, Rustici refused to work with anyone except Leonardo, and the two artists probably designed and executed the statues together. Leonardo's contributions to the sculpture are evident in several areas, especially in the hand and finger positions of St. John. Similar positioning can be seen in other Da Vinci works, such as his painting *St. John the Baptist*, created between 1513 and 1516. The finger pointing is nearly identical to that seen in the San Giovanni sculpture. It is also quite similar, in this respect, to another one of Leonardo's probable paintings, *St. John in the Wilderness*, which dates from 1510 to 1515.

29

A horse is a horse, of course, of course

Whether it's yard gnomes, porcelain Santas, or pink flamingos, most of us appreciate some form of small outdoor sculpture. In 1483, Leonardo set about creating the largest statue the world had ever seen. His personal mammoth was a design for an oversized equestrian *Statue of Francesco Sforza*, mentioned in the previous point. This grand project was begun in honor of Francesco Sforza, the father of Ludovico Sforza, Duke of Milan. At more than twenty-four feet high, the statue would have been enormous.

As explained in number 27, sculpture was never Leonardo's favorite art. But this particular project probably interested Leonardo because of his fascination with nature and animals, especially horses. While this design was a Leonardo original, the notion of capturing a battle scene in sculpture definitely had precedents in Roman and Medieval artwork, and Leonardo probably took cues from the Roman statue of Marcus Aurelius.

While Leonardo had created many sketches and variations of the design by the early 1490s, he still hadn't built an actual statue. At this point, his patrons were getting impatient, so Leonardo had to hurry and create a full-scale clay model. It was quite a hit and was set up in the garden of the Palazzo Vecchio. People traveled from all over to see this enormous masterpiece, affectionately dubbed "Il Colosso."

The clay model did wonders for Leonardo's reputation. People all over Italy knew him as that crazy artist who'd made the fantastic tribute to the Sforza family. The final bronze statue should have been one of Leonardo da Vinci's crowning achievements. He even had to design special furnaces for the bronze casting, since none of the existing furnaces was even close to being large enough.

Despite the design's immense popularity, it is not certain that this statue ever really could have been built, as there was no precedent at the time for casting a hollow-shell statue (close to two inches thick) on such a large scale. Leonardo and his workshop were in the middle of obtaining bronze (no small task for a statue that would have weighed more than sixty tons) when warfare demands intervened. France was invading Milan, and the bronze Leonardo would have used for the statue was cast into military equipment, such as cannons.

Adding insult to injury, Leonardo's treasured clay model didn't even survive the war. As the French encroached on Milan in 1499, French soldiers set up outposts near the Palazzo Vecchio. The clay horse statue was destroyed when the French used it for target practice! The bits that remained degraded slowly over time, and nothing of the original is left today.

Draw up a chair!

Renaissance art paid homage to its Greek and Roman ancestors, but at the same time forged its own path. It wasn't enough to copy the classics; Renaissance artists went one better! Different methods of artistic representation were developed during the fifteenth and sixteenth centuries, and Leonardo popularized several of them, establishing gold medal standards that future artists would emulate.

One of the most enduring innovations in Renaissance drawing was the notion of linear perspective. The concept of perspective involves the idea that it's possible to represent a three-dimensional shape (such as an apple or building) on a two-dimensional piece of paper or canvas. Sounds simple, but that's because we take it for granted today. Leon Battista Alberti (1404–1472) devised a mathematical model for drawing in perspective, where the artist pretended to draw as if through a window. This method made use of a "horizon line," which represented eye-level, and used "vanishing points" that served as connection points for all lines of sight. These points helped to designate locations for all objects in the scene. Artists drew "visual rays" from vanishing points, and through these rays, they could create objects composed of right angles (such as walls, bricks, or anything else with a sharp edge).

One-point perspective (which, as the name suggests, contains one vanishing point) was useful for scenes that looked down a narrow corridor or alley. Leonardo's *The Last Supper* is an excellent example of an interior scene that used this type of linear perspective. Two-point perspective was incorporated more often for landscapes and other scenes that contained wide angles of view. Early Renaissance architects such as Brunelleschi and Alberti worked with linear-perspective techniques, and Leonardo was a major proponent of this new drawing method.

In learning how to construct precise, accurate perspective drawings, Leonardo may have worked with a device called a perspectograph. The idea behind it was similar to a mechanic's workbench, only it was for drawing. This system involved a table with a stand that had a cutout, through which the artist could trace perspective lines of objects beyond the stand. While Leonardo didn't invent the idea of drawing in perspective, he used it to such an extent that other artists soon came to admire, and then imitate, his style.

Leonardo was actually increasing his workload by painting more realistically (and more three-dimensionally) than his predecessors. With this new way of drawing, he had to develop new techniques to make the entire painting appear more convincing. No longer would simple, flat colors suffice! Figures seen in the round had to be properly distinguished, both as their own forms and as objects distinct from the scene's background. Thus, historians largely credit Leonardo with developing another critical artistic innovation known as *chiaroscuro*, which, translated from Italian, means "clear/light and dark." Leonardo used light and dark colors to portray both shade and shadow more convincingly, as they were actually experienced in real life. This use of the *chiaroscuro* technique represented the first time a Renaissance painter had contrasted lights and darks to help create a truly three-dimensional image. *Chiaroscuro* is evident in many of Leonardo's paintings, including the early *Benois Madonna* of 1478. Leonardo's *chiaroscuro* technique has become so integral to artistic training that some historians have even called it one of Leonardo's most important artistic contributions.

In addition to representing lights and shadows accurately, realistic paintings need to convey subtle transitions from one tone to another. *Sfumato*, an Italian word meaning "vanished," is used to describe a technique Leonardo developed to do exactly that: graduate color values between parts of an object to make it accurately reflect the object's full roundness. Early Flemish painters had experimented with these methods, but none had used the technique to the same extent or with as much success as Leonardo.

The *Mona Lisa* is an excellent example of *sfumato*. While the woman's face is fully enveloped by shade and shadow, it is also completely smooth. Leonardo used brushes, as well as his fingers, to blend the tones and create perfect transitions to represent light as it swept around the woman's head. Then, the light in the scene simply subsides into darkness. The transitions between light and dark here are imperceptible; the superb blending allows viewers to focus on the painted subject, rather than the technique of painting.

The scene behind the scene

In the classical period of ancient Greece and Rome, art focused on celebrating the gods. The Renaissance brought out a new tradition of naturalistic art, one that placed religious scenes or even portraits in natural surroundings. Subtly woven into many of these works was the idea that it was possible to represent the presence of a supreme being, while simultaneously paying attention to the individual. Many of Leonardo's paintings were religious in nature, and the Renaissance's focus on humanism gave Leonardo the opportunity to incorporate his fondness for the natural world into the preexisting influence of Christianity.

Leonardo took this developing Renaissance methodology to a new level. Many of his works include fantastic landscapes as backgrounds, and these backgrounds sometimes involve complex architectural creations (think Escher) or landscapes with natural elements such as rolling hills, valleys, streams, and mountains. Yet even these more natural elements take on an air of the ethereal thanks to Leonardo's innovative techniques.

So how did Leonardo achieve these effects? His conceptual method involved rendering scenes as if they appeared through a fine veil of mist. An early precursor of this technique, called *sfumato* (see number 30), is actually visible in his earliest remaining landscape drawing, created in 1473 when Leonardo was only twenty-one. Details of this landscape seem to recede into the distance thanks to atmospheric perspective.

Perhaps the most famous of Leonardo's background landscapes is in the *Mona Lisa*. Rather than placing her indoors, as was typical for most portraits, Leonardo positioned Lisa, the woman with the enigmatic smile, in front of a dreamlike landscape full of craggy mountains and sinuous streams. The background's movement captures Leonardo's view of the natural world, one that is ever-changing and constantly in motion. The only man-made element in this background is a small bridge crossing one of the rivers. If you were to inspect the background closely, you'd also see that the two sides do not match up—the horizon on the right side of the figure is significantly higher than that on the left side. Most likely, this was a deliberate trick on Leonardo's part to lend an increased sense of activity and realism to the central figure by making her place in the painting appear to change depending on whether you look at her from the left side or from the right.

A late painting, *St. John in the Wilderness* (attributed to Leonardo, although not confirmed as his), goes one better. It combines a realistic natural setting (trees, roots, cliffs, and animals) with one of Leonardo's traditional misty backgrounds. Toward the top left of the painting, the landscape recedes into mists and lakes—very surreal. An earlier painting, *The Virgin of the Rocks*, creates a fantastic setting for a typical religious theme, placing the subjects in a cave, or grotto. The scene is complete with a reflective pool of water, gorgeous plants, and a background of rocks that erupt from the floor and hang dangerously from the ceiling. Rather than receding into darkness, the rocks extend into a bright misty region typical of Leonardo's other backgrounds.

Finish that painting!
Leonardo and the fine art of completion

While no one would ever question Leonardo's overall genius, doesn't it seem strange that we celebrate him so much as an artist, while so few of his paintings remain today? As mentioned previously, one reason for this conspicuous lack was Leonardo's tendency to start many projects, but actually finish very few. Even in his earliest days, he flitted from subject to subject, learning and experimenting with writing, drawing, painting, sculpting, music, science, engineering, and math. So why didn't he just focus on one art form? It's possible that as stunning as his works were, they did not match the perfection of the images in his head, and he gave up rather than fail in the expression of his imagined perfection. Another possibility is that, especially later in life, Leonardo saw himself more as an inventor and scientist than as an artist, and thus devoted more time to such works. The inevitable consequence was that he ended up neglecting his art.

Leonardo was an innovator, and as such, he wanted to rush out and test newly discovered techniques—which, of course, went against the tried-and-true methods of his time. Granted, his innovative approach sometimes had disastrous results. Take, for instance, his fresco *The Last Supper*. Leonardo painted this masterpiece using a new technique he'd developed, but the paint began to peel from the wall almost immediately. Another ambitious later work, *The Battle of Anghiari*, was supposed to have presented an entire battle scene on a wall opposite a new work by Michelangelo. When Leonardo actually painted the work, again using a new experimental technique, the paint adhered to the walls without problem this time. Unfortunately, when Leonardo applied heat to dry and fix the paint, his luck ran out. Some of the paint ran off the walls and the rest scaled off in pieces. The project was almost a complete failure, and other artists actually wound up painting over what remained of Leonardo's original work.

Beyond his penchant for experimentation (which sometimes backfired), perhaps Leonardo simply got bored. Maybe he worked first and most intensely on the aspects of a painting that he found most interesting: the design and rendering of faces, hands, hair, and background landscapes. Once he was finished with those portions, he may have simply left other parts of his paintings incomplete or had his students fill in certain elements, which seems to be the case with his *Portrait of a Musician*. Leonardo rendered the face and hands exquisitely, but he barely sketched the drapery of the young man's tunic into place.

Not finishing what he started got Leonardo into trouble on more than one occasion. In some cases, patrons never paid him for his unfinished work; in other cases, he had to return the initial advance money he received when he didn't complete a painting on time. For example, despite having a contract, Leonardo never completed *Adoration of the Magi*, meant for the monks at Scopeto in 1481. Apparently, Leonardo only finished a sketch and never even started the main painting. A lawsuit over another work, *The Virgin of the Rocks*, dragged on for about ten years. As a result, Leonardo eventually completed two versions of the painting to fulfill the contract.

The equestrian *Statue of Francesco Sforza* is yet another work that, although ambitious in creative scope, perhaps overreached the realm of feasibility (see number 29). If Leonardo had been willing to settle for a smaller sculpture—life-sized for instance—the statue might have been built and probably would have survived the battles in Renaissance Italy. However, settling doesn't seem to have been in Leonardo's nature. He designed this sculpture to stand more than twenty-five feet tall and, as a result, he ran into problems. For starters, there was no foundry big enough to create such a large sculpture. Then, as he was gathering bronze to cast the sculpture, Milan became embroiled in war and Leonardo had to surrender his precious supplies for military usage. Leonardo had only a clay model of the horse statue to show for all of his efforts, and that was eventually destroyed when the French used it for target practice.

Although Leonardo's failure to complete so many of his works might lead you to believe otherwise, at times he was quite a perfectionist, refusing to let go of certain works to which he felt particularly attached. The *Mona Lisa* is a perfect example of this; Leonardo moved his favorite painting around with him from studio to studio, working and reworking it for many years, until near the end of his life. In fact, he never really judged this painting finished.

Building the scene-scape

The advent of humanism brought plenty of changes to Renaissance artists and patrons. Artists like Leonardo had to develop new techniques and skills to paint increasingly convincing scenes—people expected more, and artists had to live up to those expectations. Fortunately, Leonardo excelled at incorporating nature and landscapes into his paintings. He spent much time studying anatomy, biology, and geology, and his observations gave him a keen sense of proportion and movement.

Along with this interest in humanism, architectural landscapes also became increasingly popular during the Renaissance. As this idea was a relatively new addition to Leonardo's artistic bag of tricks, some of his early examples seem awkward or forced. The *Dreyfuss Madonna* of 1469 demonstrates this problem quite well. The Madonna is seated in front of a window, which is too close to the viewer to be properly discernable. Its rendering is too dark in contrast to the brightness of the Madonna in the foreground, and it appears out of place. The landscape seen through the window seems equally disjointed. Despite questions about its execution, this painting is important because it represents one of Leonardo's early attempts to create coherence amongst natural, built, and human forms.

From 1472 to 1475, Leonardo contributed to at least one version of an Annunciation scene. This painting features many architectural elements, including a marble sarcophagus representing a Medici family tomb. The composition appears awkward, and not all of the figures are drawn in the same perspective (the Virgin Mary is posed in a three-quarter view, whereas an angel is depicted almost sideways). Nevertheless, this painting has much more pronounced architectural definition than Leonardo's previous works. There is a partially revealed doorway, and the wall behind it is defined with enormous quoins. This sort of precise architectural detailing was without classical precedent, and even artist-architects such as Brunelleschi and Alberti did not present built elements to such an extent. The landscape in the background appears nearly flat, however, indicating that Leonardo still had some refining to do when it came to working out the coordination of nature and architecture fully.

Madonna of the Carnation is another interior scene that deals with the background in a more three-dimensional way. This painting dates to 1478, and you can easily see Leonardo's increasing expertise with perspective. The arched colonnade clearly shows one-point perspective, though the angle of view is somewhat inconsistent with the perspective of the foreground figures.

The Last Supper, completed in 1498, combines the best of both worlds: humanlike figures with real architectural interiors. Leonardo used single-point perspective to create a space that was geometrically precise. Most of the painting is also symmetrical, showing off the latent influence of classical notions of balance and proportion. The upper part of the image (before restoration) actually shows imperfect symmetry and slightly off-center perspective. Leonardo found a way to sneak in his own special touch through these small sorts of details.

An architecture of the imagination

As if creating some of the first Renaissance architectural paintings wasn't enough, Leonardo also painted scenes that demonstrated a sort of "faux architecture." This term might sound odd, but bear with us. These works contained architectural elements that had more in common with flights of fancy than with anything rooted in concrete reality. The *Adoration of the Magi* of 1481 is one of the best examples. Commissioned for the monastery at San Donato Scopeto, Leonardo worked on this scene during his years under Lorenzo de Medici, and it was the first work that he created largely on his own. While the painting focuses on Mary, the baby Jesus, and the three Magi, the scene also contains about sixty other people, a variety of animals, and other natural elements.

Although Leonardo never finished this painting, it is clear that the scene contains architectural elements that were, at least partially, more imaginary than real. Take, for example, the staircase depicted in the background. It could be part of a medieval castle, or maybe it belongs to the ruins of a Roman imperial palace. Either way, these structures would have been completely out of place for this religious scene set in a lush countryside—not the best place to build a castle, which surely would have required at least basic defenses.

The scene is a fanciful composition, to be sure. Its early sketches were even wilder, showing animals in different perspectives and poses. Some sketches had parts of the stairs dating from a different period and age; some were even composed of different materials. It was a motley crüe of painting, and Leonardo probably loved painting every minute of it. There are multiple points of perspective, and the scene almost looks more like a collage than one coherent painting.

Perhaps Leonardo's playful side came to the fore through these sorts of details, or maybe they afforded Leonardo the opportunity to contrast his new skills against a more whimsical background. Whatever the reason, the fanciful architecture incorporated within Leonardo's paintings increases the depth of his work and speaks to both his inherent creativity and his willingness to take risks.

35

It's all in the details

Leonardo had a knack for capturing facial expressions, and you can see that even in his early works. *Lady with an Ermine*, painted around 1490 (or perhaps earlier), is a portrait of Cecilia Gallerani, the young mistress of Duke Ludovico Sforza. Often called the first modern portrait, this work is much different than established methods of portrait painting in the fifteenth century. Leonardo posed Cecilia in three-quarter view, rather than in the strict profile view favored at the time. There's also an added sense of motion inherent in this scene, as she twists her head and upper body, fixing her gaze on something outside the field of view. The warm lighting provides a three-dimensional look that has an almost sculptural effect. The painting also renders the detailed embroidery and ribbons on Cecilia's gown with painstaking precision. The beauty of Cecilia's face, and her enigmatic half-smile, evoke a later (and more famous) portrait—the *Mona Lisa*.

Another one of Da Vinci's famous faces is found in his *Portrait of Ginevra de'Benci* which could date to as early as 1474, when Leonardo was still working with Verrocchio. It includes some elements typical of Leonardo's style, such as a mystical backdrop and detailed background rendering, and it also shows botanical elements, such as the juniper bush. The portrait itself is much flatter and has none of the three-dimensionality of *Lady with an Ermine* or some of Leonardo's other later works. However, her face and skin do have that marble appearance found in Leonardo's later works, and the emphasis on the ringlets of her hair is also typical Leonardo.

Another early work, *Portrait of a Musician*, dates from around the same period (1482–1483). However, attributing this painting to Leonardo is problematic—there are no records mentioning the painting, nor is there any documentation for its commission. The painting has some elements of Leonardo's style, but one of his students could also have been the artist—the likeliest suspects include Bernardino Luini, Giovanni Boltraffio, and Ambrogio de Predis.

So what's the proof of Leonardo's influence here? For starters, you can look at the shadowed background, the length of the figure, and the three-quarter view of the subject. But that's not all. The delicate bone structure required detailed knowledge of anatomy, and Leonardo was one of only a handful of painters who had that skill. Then there's the subject's casual, unforced pose, delicate fingers, and curling hair. All of these details point to Leonardo. This painting also remained unfinished, and various elements are only sketched in—and who was our favorite artist known for leaving works half done? None other than Leonardo!

Monks and lawyers and artists, oh my!

Who would've thought that Leonardo had a legal run-in with Catholic monks? That's exactly what happened with *The Virgin of the Rocks*. In fact, this project was actually done twice because of the lawsuit that ensued!

The chapel of the Immaculata at the church of San Francesco Grande, in Milan, originally commissioned *The Virgin of the Rocks* in 1483 as an altarpiece. One of Leonardo's first commissions in Milan, the painting relates to the Immaculate Conception, the Catholic Church's teaching that Mary was conceived without original sin. The Italian papacy charged Leonardo with the task of portraying the Virgin in a pure, holy, and innocent manner.

The original contract was very specific, spelling out the exact subject of the picture. The premise seems straightforward enough: The monks of San Francesco wanted the Virgin to be the painting's central focus, with prototypical Greek angels flanking her. Leonardo designed his work to fit into a panel, which would have been framed by painted or gilded shutters. Evangelista and Ambrogio de Predis were to complete the surrounding work. Details of the background (mountains and rocks) were also laid out before Leonardo began work on the project. The original contract even called for specifics on the Virgin and angels' robe colors! Despite all of the specifics, Leonardo did take some artistic license. For instance, he exchanged one of the angels for St. John.

This wasn't exactly a rush job, but the contract length was short—only eight months to complete the entire painting. It was supposed to be completed prior to the Feast of the Immaculate Conception, held annually on December 8. Predictably, Leonardo ran into some trouble finishing the painting on schedule, and the work became the subject of a lengthy lawsuit. The eventual result was that two versions of the work were created—one is presently part of the Louvre's collection, while the other resides in London's National Gallery.

In addition to the missed deadline, Leonardo and de Predis apparently had a dispute with the monks about their commission. Leonardo complained to the monks that they hadn't received their full payment, and the initial amount negotiated for the entire work had barely covered the cost of the frame! Disputes and lawsuits over time and money continued for many years.

Eventually, the monks deemed the first version incomplete, thus forfeiting the rest of the money and giving Leonardo ownership of the painting. Leonardo probably gave this version as a gift to King Louis XII of France, who helped resolve the lawsuit, and this is the version that now hangs in the Louvre. Leonardo renegotiated the contract with the monks, who agreed to pay for a second version in 1506. The monks gave Leonardo and de Predis two years to complete this painting, paying them half the amount originally negotiated. This version was actually finished on time and was finally hung in the chapel on August 18, 1508. It remained there until 1781, when it passed through the hands of a number of collectors, eventually ending up in the National Gallery of London.

While Leonardo is likely the sole artist behind the Louvre version, this may not be the case with the second. The newer painting contains a few significant changes from the older version. The colors are brighter and bluer, the angel on the right is no longer pointing at St. John (who is now holding a cross), and halos have been added above the Virgin Mary and one of the angels. Leonardo probably supervised the creation of this second painting, but it is likely that other artists in his studio did the actual painting.

The life and times of *The Last Supper*

One of Leonardo's signature paintings, *The Last Supper* is also one of the most accident-prone and least well preserved. Leonardo completed this giant wall painting in 1498. It depicts the moment at which Jesus announces that one of his disciples is going to betray him (ultimately, it is Judas).

Duke Ludovico Sforza, Leonardo's patron at the time, commissioned the painting. Sforza had selected the Church of Santa Maria delle Grazie as his family chapel, and Leonardo was hired to paint a large mural of the Last Supper on one wall of the refectory (a room where meals are served). Although the work was to be done on a grand scale—thirty feet long and fourteen feet high—Leonardo was not one to turn down a challenge.

Leonardo completed *The Last Supper,* certainly one of his great masterpieces, in only three years. This time scale seems especially miraculous when compared to many of Leonardo's other projects, which either were never completed or dragged on for many years.

The work's design is one of Leonardo's most innovative. The perspective makes the painting appear to be a logical extension of the room, with the eye invariably drawn to the head of Christ at the center. The Apostles are crowded around the table in natural poses, in contrast to the stiff appearance of most versions of this scene during Leonardo's time.

Each Apostle has a distinctive appearance and character. Apparently, Leonardo modeled each of their faces on a particular individual. The two main figures, Judas and Christ, gave Leonardo the greatest difficulty. Christ's expression, a model of serenity, is a dramatic contrast to the Apostles' stunned and conflicted faces.

One legend tells of Leonardo's difficulty with modeling Judas, Jesus' betrayer. Supposedly, the chapel's prior complained about how long the painting was taking, and Leonardo retorted it was because he was lacking a model for Judas, but the prior seemed to him a good candidate! Leonardo got away with this slight, but luckily doesn't seem to have made a habit of it.

Leonardo worked on *The Last Supper* in his characteristic style. Days of frantic work, during which Leonardo worked all day without stopping, were followed by days during which Leonardo was not seen at all. After being absent for several days, he would sometimes appear, gaze silently at the painting for several hours, excitedly add a few brush strokes, and then disappear again. Leonardo did eventually finish the work, however, and the public immediately recognized it as a masterpiece.

So all was well—Leonardo finished this sacred artwork and everyone was happy. Right? Unfortunately, *The Last Supper* began to deteriorate almost as soon as it was finished, once again due to Leonardo's love of innovations. Instead of using the usual method of fresco painting, in which paint was applied to a wall of fresh, wet plaster, Leonardo designed a new method where he applied paint directly to dry plaster. This method let him work much more slowly and methodically and allowed a wider range of colors and tones in the paint. Unfortunately, that's where the good news stopped. This method proved unstable, and the paint began flaking off the wall during Leonardo's lifetime.

By 1586, the masterpiece had degraded to such an extent that it was hardly visible. Over the years, a number of attempts were made to restore the painting. Unfortunately, these methods often caused more harm than good, or they involved so much overpainting that little of Leonardo's masterpiece remained visible.

The work also suffered from more practical concerns in the church. At one point, workers cut a door opening through the bottom of the image—at the expense of Christ's feet, which were removed because of it. In 1796, Napoleon's troops even used the room containing the painting as a stable, of all things! After that, *The Last Supper* still had more than its share of disasters to endure. A flood in 1800 left it covered in a layer of green mold, and Allied bombing in 1943 blew the ceiling off the church rectory. Given this tumultuous history, it's surprising anything is left of *The Last Supper* at all!

An initial restoration was completed in 1954, and finally a twenty-two-year-long project was completed in 1999. The restoration attempted to remove centuries' worth of preservation and repainting, to reveal Leonardo's original intent. The process was truly painstaking, requiring restorers to reattach tiny flakes of the original paint in their original locations. Unfortunately, parts of the work are beyond repair, including the facial expressions of the Apostles. However, a number of copies exist, some dating from before the deterioration had become problematic. If you compare these views to the currently restored version, you can imagine how spectacular the original of *The Last Supper* must have been right after it was painted.

There's something about Lisa

Just about everyone knows the *Mona Lisa*—it's the painting for which Leonardo da Vinci is, perhaps, most famous. Completed in 1506, this work of art went through a number of iterations before the design and execution were finally finished. What is it about this particular piece that has created such a lasting impact on the artistic world?

The subject of the *Mona Lisa* was most likely the wife of Francesco del Giocondo. A silk merchant in the late fifteenth century, Giocondo was also involved with the government in Florence, and he and his wife Lisa were probably married around 1495. The portrait poses Lisa as a pyramidal foreground to a distant, somewhat foggy landscape in the background. The glow on her chest radiates to include her face and hands, creating a softness not previously seen in Renaissance painting. This painting was much smaller than many of Leonardo's other works. It measures approximately 30″ × 40″ and consists of oil paint on a wooden panel.

With the *Mona Lisa*, Leonardo made profound use of the techniques he had developed throughout the Renaissance. The soft transitions between colors (*sfumato*) create a fully realistic three-dimensional figure with amazing modeling of the skin. Leonardo used the same techniques in the background—the sky and water complement each other perfectly. Similarly, the use of contrasting light for shade and shadow (*chiaroscuro*) creates a connection between the curves of Lisa's face and hair, and the mountains behind her.

While it appears that the figure of Lisa is floating in front of the landscape, in the original painting she is actually standing in between two columns, probably on a porch or balcony. Because these elements were removed from the final version, viewers today cannot experience the painting as it was initially intended.

The expression on this Florentine woman's face is one of the painting's most exceptional features. Her simple, dark clothing makes her face the real focus. Her smile appears to be at once both innocent and enticing. One account describes how Leonardo had to hire musicians and mimes to amuse Lisa during the sitting—after all, three years is a long time to pose! The entertainment could provide one explanation for Lisa's slight smile. Also significant about Lisa's expression is that one eye is slightly higher than the other, increasing the sense of movement in the painting. If you've ever seen the *Mona Lisa* in person, you know that her eyes seem to follow you around the room. Leonardo probably created this effect on purpose. The corners of the mouth and eyes are the most expressive parts of the human face, and Leonardo did not overdefine these parts of the *Mona Lisa*. Instead, they are highly shadowed and almost vague, causing her expression to appear to change depending on the viewer's perspective.

Like Leonardo himself, the *Mona Lisa* did plenty of traveling. Leonardo carried it with him to France during his tenure under King François I. At the end of his life he either gave or sold it to the King, and it eventually ended up in the Louvre. Napoleon borrowed the painting for a period, and it was hidden during the Franco-Prussian War to ensure it wasn't stolen or damaged. In 1911, a Louvre employee named Vincenzo Peruggia stole the painting and then tried to sell it, but he was captured and the artwork was returned to the Louvre in 1913.

The *Mona Lisa* was hidden again during World Wars I and II. Then, it toured various countries (including the United States) during the 1960s and 1970s. Unfortunately, due to security concerns, it's unlikely that it will leave the Louvre again any time soon. At present, it resides in the museum behind bulletproof glass in a climate-controlled enclosure.

39

Oldies but goodies

While his early work is probably his most famous, Leonardo made many paintings later in life that would become popular in their own right. One of Leonardo's last works, *The Virgin and Child with Saint Anne* is one of his most celebrated. Leonardo first explored this somewhat obscure religious theme in a sketch done in 1498. The basic layout of the scene contained the Virgin Mary with her mother, Saint Anne, and the infant Christ. Although that early sketch has been lost, a later one, dubbed the "Burlington House Cartoon" (named after a former British owner's collection), shows a discarded concept for this work. In fact, this sketch is sometimes preferred over the finished painting!

During the Renaissance, a "cartoon" referred to a full-sized sketch that showed the planned layout of a painting, which the artist then transferred to the canvas or panel to be actually painted. The Burlington House Cartoon shows the infant Christ blessing a young St. John, accompanied by Mary and Anne. Leonardo abandoned this concept for unknown reasons and never actually painted it, but when the sketch was exhibited, it received major acclaim. This sketch is still celebrated as one of Leonardo's major works. The facial expressions and poses are considered much more natural than those in the completed painting.

The monks of the Florentine Santissima Annunziata commissioned the version of *The Virgin and Child with Saint Anne* that Leonardo actually did paint as an altarpiece for their high altar. Leonardo completed the work, which dates from 1507–1513, in his typical fashion: not on time. The monks, eager for their new work, had to commission another piece. In fact, they had given the original commission to Filippino Lippi, but he rejected the project, suggesting that the monks give the commission to Leonardo (whom he considered a superior artist). When Leonardo failed to complete the work on time, Lippi took on the project, but he died before finishing his work. The monks finally got their painting when Perugino completed Lippi's work.

Leonardo's painting of *The Virgin and Child with Saint Anne*, completed well past the monks' deadline, shows Mary seated on her mother Anne's lap. Mary is leaning over to her infant son, who is holding a lamb. (The lamb represents a symbol of what Jesus would become: a sacrifice.) Anne's face is peaceful and serene, while Mary's suggests resignation, as if she realizes the fate for which her infant son is destined. She almost restrains Christ from embracing the lamb, and therefore his destiny, yet she also seems to have accepted his role.

The painting's composition is balanced and fluid, although some critics have remarked that the poses seem awkward. Leonardo positioned Mary and

Jesus' arms like links on a chain, links that span multiple generations. The background of the painting includes a typically Leonardo-esque wilderness, complete with hazy, impassible mountain peaks, and meandering rivers. The tree in the near background is more earthly than the misty background, but rendered with Leonardo's signature botanical precision.

Like so many of Leonardo's paintings, Leonardo left *The Virgin and Child with Saint Anne* unfinished. Careful examination of the painting has suggested that Leonardo himself painted the background and the three figures, while it's likely that one of Leonardo's students completed the rest of the painting, including the lamb and the drapery covering the Virgin's legs. Unlike many of Leonardo's paintings, which he worked and reworked, the paint on this one is of variable thickness, and the sketch lines beneath the paint are visible in places.

Leonardo painted his final work, *St. John the Baptist*, during his last years in Rome, between approximately 1509 and 1516. It's quite an unusual treatment of the subject. Scripture portrays St. John the Baptist as a gaunt creature living in the wilderness. The way Leonardo painted him, however, St. John looks almost womanly. He has Leonardo's signature long, flowing, curly locks, a demurely bent arm, and an enigmatic smile quite similar to Mona Lisa's.

Unlike most of Leonardo's paintings, there is no mystical background behind St. John. Rather, the painting shows a mysterious darkness from which a glowing figure emerges. A different artist likely painted the cross that St. John holds and the animal skin he wears, and it's possible that the same unknown artist darkened the background as well. *St. John the Baptist* was widely copied by Leonardo's students, and a number of these copies exist with questionable attributions.

Building the Renaissance

Leonardo da Vinci was not a practicing architect, though he spent years studying mathematics, urban design, and civil engineering. He designed military structures, buildings, and other architectural objects. Even though none of his designs were constructed during his lifetime, he was amazingly prolific. Leonardo's voluminous drawings, sketches, writings, paintings, and other artwork reveal his architectural achievements.

Though not trained in architecture, Leonardo was familiar with architectural drawings.

In addition to learning the language of architects, Leonardo used the perspective techniques he developed in painting to represent his designs for palaces, churches, cityscapes, and other projects. Particularly with landscapes, Leonardo was fond of drawing "bird's-eye perspectives." While typical eye-level perspectives were drawn as someone on the ground would see them, aerial views showed a project in its entirety, including the surrounding areas. Along with Michelangelo and Raphael, Leonardo was one of the first Renaissance architects to make use of this technique.

Fillippo Brunelleschi (1377–1446) provided an early architectural model, one that Leonardo continued into the Renaissance. Brunelleschi was one of the first architects to seize upon classical foundations in the creation of a modern architecture that could rival that of its ancestors. He designed churches such as

San Lorenzo and San Spirito, which were based on Roman ideals of balance, harmony, and proportion. Leonardo took those ideas under advisement in many of his own architectural designs.

Genius doesn't simply appear out of thin air; even masters such as Leonardo had to build their experience (and reputation!) on the success of others. Leonardo's main sources of architectural inspiration were probably Alberti, Bramante, and Raphael. Leon Batista Alberti (1406–1472), an architect, artist, composer, and author, was responsible for writing the Renaissance's first treatise on architecture. He based his designs on classical architecture, and it is likely that Leonardo studied Alberti's designs during his apprenticeship to Verrocchio. Donato Bramante (1444–1514) was another primary Renaissance architect. As an official architect for Pope Julius II, he created masterpieces in the style of Greek and Roman classics, interpreting them in light of Renaissance Christian teachings. Raphael (1483–1520) followed in Bramante's footsteps by becoming the next papal architect. He was known for adhering to a fairly strict system of classical spatial organization. Raphael was also a distinguished artist. As you can see, there was clearly no lack of architectural talent during the Renaissance!

While synthesis of form and structure can be a goal for many architects, it is not a given. As both an artist and a student of mathematics, however, Leonardo had the distinct advantage of being able to conceptualize a project in its entirety. He was interested in appearance, as well as structure and construction. Leonardo's talent for encompassing both areas in his studies set him apart from many of his predecessors and paved the way for more modern ways of thinking about architectural design.

The Milan dome

During his major period in Milan (1482–1499), Leonardo was busy with assignments from his patron Ludovico Sforza, the Duke of Milan. His major artistic accomplishments during this time include *The Virgin of the Rocks* and *The Last Supper*, paintings that earned an esteemed place in history for their beauty, innovation, and highly skilled production. This was also a time of major experimentation for Leonardo—he produced paintings, sketches of military equipment, sculptures, machinery prototypes, and architectural designs.

One of Leonardo's most significant ventures in architecture occurred in 1488, when he created a preliminary design for the dome and tambour of the Milan Gothic Cathedral. This massive cathedral was a huge undertaking, not just for Milan but for much of Italy. Built over a 500-year period, the cathedral brought the High Gothic style to Milan at quite a price. It is the central focus of town, with most streets ending at its doors. Work on the cathedral began in 1387. As political and religious power continued to change hands over the years, new designers and master masons were invited to work on the cathedral, which would be a living tribute to the creativity of Italian artists. Political and financial messes slowed down the project, though, and the great spire wasn't constructed until the mid–eighteenth century; additional spires and stair towers were built during the nineteenth century. By this point, some of the original work was already crumbling! Restoration was necessary, and that task occupied much of the early twentieth century.

During the end of the fifteenth century, the Sforza and Solari families exerted strong Tuscan influence over the cathedral's design (see number 21 for more on the Sforzas). The Solari family, based in Milan, included many artists and architects whose designs were prominent all over Italy. Giovanni Amadeo was slated to design the drum of the Milan cathedral, and despite the burgeoning presence of Renaissance architecture, he was determined to keep a strong tie to the site's Gothic roots.

Around this time, Leonardo da Vinci was consulted regarding several aspects of the cathedral. As usual, he wanted to involve himself in as many projects as possible, so he submitted drawings for the dome. Even though it was never built, Leonardo's design for the dome was an important marker in his career since, at this point, he was starting to incorporate studies of mathematics (particularly geometry) into his designs.

This project also brings to light Leonardo's famed multitasking. For example, Leonardo produced designs for several types of construction equipment, and his ideas for cranes were particularly useful for this dome project.

Order in the church!

The history of church design is a long and rich one. Religious structures are typically more permanent (and more respected) than any other type of building. Despite political and social turmoil, ecclesiastical architecture tends to survive. Ancient Athenians devoted their entire lives to constructing the Acropolis; the Parthenon, the Erechtheion, and other Greek temples were models of religious fervor coupled with civic pride. The Romans built arches and monuments for their emperors who, many Romans believed, had ties to the gods themselves. Medieval French architecture, as demonstrated by Chartres Cathedral and others, celebrated Catholicism with amazing feats of Gothic engineering. Across time, culture, and geography, churches and other religious edifices have provided opportunity for social consciousness and pride; they've also fascinated designers. Church designs were of particularly high importance because of their enduring influence. Is it any surprise that they interested Leonardo?

During the Renaissance, the principles of architecture were crystallized into treatises. Leonardo most likely read and studied these works, and the strict series of rules they presented probably influenced his rigorous church designs. Leon Battista Alberti's *On the Art of Building in Ten Books* (first published in 1485) is worthy of particular note here. This manifesto defined both symbols and usage, and was central to changing the perception of architecture from a craft into a true profession. Leonardo must have studied this work, because his sketches of religious architecture embody many of its principles.

Through his drawing, painting, and architecture, Leonardo was devoted to showing the order and articulation beyond what was visible. In the 1480s, Leonardo made pages and pages worth of sketches for various church designs. His notebooks include designs for multilevel structures and churches with domes, but he seems to have experimented most intensely with the central-plan church. (Brunelleschi's churches made use of the central-plan design, and his designs probably influenced Leonardo.)

The basic idea for the central-plan design involved a focal point for the church—a square, circle, or some other variant—from which other rooms radiated outward. Leonardo made many sketches of the Greek cross, a three-dimensional cross shape where all legs were of equal size. His drawings are filled with complex geometrical interaction based on the idea of a modular unit that was repeated and combined with other identical units. Proportions, directly derived from formal mathematical relationships, were also key in his designs.

While Leonardo's various church designs were never actually constructed, they are significant because they provided inspiration for later Renaissance architects. Bramante in particular probably studied Da Vinci's church sketches; several of his churches show evidence of Leonardo's classical sense of proportion and form.

San Giovanni Church: Closer to heaven

Renaissance Florence was historically a family-run town. Powerful families dominated each region, and the Florentine system of government was more or less an oligarchy. By 1343, the city was divided into sections, or quarters: Santa Croce, Santa Maria Novella, Santo Spirito, and San Giovanni. Each quarter had its say in nominating officials and would eventually have a major church supporting its saint. Leonardo became involved with the design of the church of San Giovanni.

This church has enormous cultural significance for Florentines. In addition to housing a number of sculptural masterpieces, it's rumored that several famous Italian artists and authors were baptized here, including Dante.

The Baptistery of San Giovanni, located in what is known today as the Piazza San Giovanni, was a crowning achievement. It was created and named for the patron saint of Florence, St. John the Baptist (San Giovanni in Italian). Workers began construction on this building in the eleventh and twelfth centuries, and hundreds of years later it was still going strong. The basic design is an octagonal structure faced with white and green marble. The most famous parts of the Baptistery are the bronze doors on the eastern side. These doors would eventually contain a number of sculptural scenes from the Bible. Their first designer, Andrea da Pontedera, worked on this project in the 1330s. This was the first time artists had attempted to cast sculptural bronze at this scale. At twenty-eight panels total, it was also a very large job!

A competition was held in the early fifteenth century for sculptural panels on a new set of baptistery doors. Lorenzo Ghiberti beat out Brunelleschi for this honor, and saw his panels hung in 1424. Ghiberti received the honor of creating the remainder of the work, and this project kept his shop busy well into the 1450s.

Although he wasn't involved in the design, Leonardo probably played an advisory role during the creation of the sculptural doors. In the winter of 1507, he was called to Florence to aid a sculptor, Giovanni Francesco Rustici (1474–1554), with a project for the Baptistery. The three bronze statues of St. John, a Pharisee, and a Levite are located on pedestals above the north doors. Judging from the sculptures' anatomical precision, Leonardo either worked on them himself, or at least developed detailed sketches for them.

But Leonardo's work on the Baptistery didn't end there. He later got involved in a second round of work that was more monumental than the first: Leonardo developed a scheme for transporting the building! Believe it or not, he actually proposed a plan to lift *and* move the entire Baptistery of San Giovanni. He had the idea that elevating the structure so that it would sit upon a marble base would make the church more authoritative and divine. Needless to say, this project would have required an enormous engineering effort.

44

Build it and they will come: Designs for other public structures

Most of Leonardo's architectural designs were for cathedrals or entire cities, but he also worked on a variety of smaller-scale public projects. Unfortunately, most of these public designs were never built. Leonardo employed his creative talents to design many public buildings with the goal of improving functionality and enhancing city dwellers' lives. He also included elements based on ideas of symmetry and balance, just like those he used in his designs for religious buildings.

Leonardo designed to extremes, even though some of his projects were more pedestrian in nature. For example, one sketch of a horse stable includes arches and columns supporting a vaulted ceiling, including three lower-level arcades and a number of air-circulating openings outside the building. Along with his design, Leonardo also included notes on how to run a fresh, orderly stable.

In one of his more elite forays, Leonardo designed a palace with a series of multileveled porticos. He designated the light and airy top levels of the palace for the upper classes, leaving the roads and paths that extended through the lower levels for the merchant classes. He reserved the roads through the base of the structure for transporting animals. The height of the palace was equivalent to the width of the streets below it, and he added porticoes and windows to improve airflow through the structure. In spite of its intricacies, Leonardo's design also had more pragmatic intentions; it was an attempt to ameliorate the narrow, crowded conditions on Milan's existing streets, which many designers and scientists of the day believed had actually contributed to the plague that killed almost a third of Milan's population between 1484 and 1486.

During his time in France with King François I, it's thought that Leonardo helped design the king's chateau, Chambord. Construction took place between 1519 and 1547, and Leonardo probably worked on initial plans for such features as a double spiral staircase. This special stair was similar to the four-ramp staircase that Leonardo had designed for a military fort (see number 45). Reportedly, the two paths of the spiral staircase allowed the king's wife to take one route, and his mistress to take another, which meant there wouldn't be any unpleasant chance encounters.

Leonardo's public projects include work he did in 1492, with Ambrogio da Cortis and Bramante, to rebuild the public marketplace in Vigevano. While today the city of Vigevano boasts that Leonardo designed their public square, in truth, it's possible that only his plans for the plaza's overall proportions were fully realized.

In 1518, Leonardo began one of his last architectural projects, studying the topography of the Loire River Valley, in France, for a royal fountain he was designing. Like so many of his other projects, however, this fountain was never built.

Military architecture, the design of defense

Military architecture today is a highly specialized field. Can you imagine a painter with no military training just hopping on a flight to Fort Bliss and putting up towers? Leonardo faced no such restrictions. During his time with Francesco Sforza in Milan, he designed buildings with various military reinforcements. His ability to design for the military endeared him to his patron—never a bad thing for an artist! One such building was a castle with a triple defense system. Between about 1487 and 1490, Leonardo sketched both a plan and a perspective drawing for one corner of this building. He made a point of showing two different angular fortifications, one extending over the corner of the fort and the other (which included a formidable moat) extending over part of the external wall.

His design included a series of cannons located on the overhanging wall, which allowed the castle defenders to shoot directly at all attacking forces. Leonardo also designed a triangle-shaped bastion, a structure that allowed the soldiers inside the fortress to defend the entrance. Leonardo's drawing for this type of structure was probably based on existing buildings, and it dates to his time in Romagna as Cesare Borgia's military engineer (between about 1501 and 1504). The design included three small structures, probably service buildings, on top of the main edifice. There were also a series of embrasures (openings for cannons) along the top wall.

But there's more. Leonardo also designed an innovative staircase for use in a fortified tower. His scheme included four different ramps. Each path was independent of the others, allowing soldiers to go up or down the four-story tower without running into groups going in the opposite direction. This technique could improve the soldiers' response times, as they would be able to move both troops and weapons quickly during an attack. Leonardo's design for this structure, probably also done between 1487 and 1490, included both a perspective view of the tower with the staircases exposed, and a top plan view.

In about 1502, Leonardo designed an addition to a moat. And no, his solution didn't involve just filling it with alligators! He did something much more interesting. He hid a cylindrical tower under the water, giving it a gently sloping roof that stuck up slightly above the water's surface. This system allowed defenders inside the moat tower to fire weapons right across the water's surface. Wet hay would cover the roof of the tower to protect against damage from incoming gunshots.

He built this city

Urban design was of major interest during the Renaissance. Of particular importance was a place for people to gather for political and social events, which gave rise to the formation of the town center. The public space, or *piazza* (plaza), was one of the most common architectural elements during the Renaissance. Add to the mixture defense towers and palaces, which were also common during the fifteenth and sixteenth centuries as key symbols of a family's wealth and influence.

Renaissance design influenced the set-up for Milan's city center, as was the case for so many other European cities. Its major structures are the Castello Sforezsco and the Duomo cathedral. Although the architects of that time were working on Renaissance-style designs, they also focused much of their energy on continued construction of projects that had begun in the medieval period, such as the Church of San Giovanni in Florence. Just like the artists of the time, Renaissance architects looked to classical Rome for inspiration, and a mandatory part of the architectural apprenticeship usually included a trip to Rome to study the ancient orders.

Somewhere alone the way, Leonardo developed a taste for urban design. His notebooks are filled with sketches of buildings, bridges, tunnels, streets, and entire cityscapes. As Milan's population grew, Leonardo sketched out a proposal for separated "satellite" cities that would surround a central core. Sounds like suburbia, doesn't it?

Leonardo based this particular idea on a concern for the health of Milan's citizens. Europe faced a number of plagues throughout history, but Milan was hit particularly hard by a series of plagues between 1484 and 1485. As a result, Leonardo started to think about a "healthy design" for an ideal city that emphasized cleanliness and hygiene. Some of Leonardo's suggestions included wider streets, more space in between buildings, and an anatomically based "circulatory system" of roads that would allow for better air passage. Applying his humanist, classical training to urban design, Leonardo came up with a system of proportion whereby city streets had to be at least as wide as the houses were tall. While Leonardo's goals of cleaning up Italy were certainly admirable, it's evident today that his schemes were inadequately engineered. Still, his sketches of separate transportation passageways for horse-drawn wagons and foot travelers prefigured developments of modern city planners.

As mentioned in number 44, Leonardo also proposed the idea for a multilevel city where workers and craftsmen would literally function beneath the wealthy, the clergy, and others with more noble stature. (How would *you* like to live under your boss's feet?) For these studies, he likely drew on his knowledge of other architects, including Alberti and Brunelleschi, who had produced similar ideas.

In 1515, Leonardo outdid himself when he submitted a plan for a combined city and palace complex to François I in Romarantin, France. This design, contained in the "Codex Arundel" (see number 72), shows bridges, canals, and a multilevel city center with underground traffic tunnels. Leonardo's design, unfortunately, was never built.

Leonardo was also a pioneer in the field of cartography, particularly in the production of accurate city maps. His map for the town of Imola, produced during his time in Florence around 1502, is thought to be one of the first geometrically precise town plans. This plan may have had strategic importance, as notes included along with the drawing contain distances and directions to various locations in Imola.

Part 3

WHAT IT'S ALL ABOUT

In addition to working on many projects related to painting and architectural design, Leonardo devoted much of his time to studying the sciences. He based his theories on observations of the natural world and then attempted to explain and understand his observations. In this regard, Leonardo was the first of the modern scientists, since his methods were a sharp contrast to the medieval world in which religious mystery cloaked science. While the "Father of Modern Medicine" title usually goes to Hippocrates, Leonardo comes in a close second.

As discussed in Part 1, Leonardo spent his childhood immersed in nature, observing and sketching what he saw. As an adult, he asked questions and sought answers to the mysteries of the world around him. His investigations led him to study anatomy and zoology. He performed detailed dissections on both animals and humans. He was also interested in botany, geology, and the behavior of water as a fluid.

Leonardo's interest in flight led him into engineering, where he invented a number of flying machines. He also spent time as a military engineer, inventing new weapons and defensive mechanisms. His other inventions ranged from improvements in the printing press to a diving apparatus that would allow swimmers to breathe under water. Many of his inventions were never built and were, in fact, beyond the technological capabilities of his time. However, some of his designs—his parachute, for instance—have been built in modern times, and they work quite well.

Observe and understand

Leonardo's scientific pursuits have earned him a firm place as the first of the true modern scientists. In fact, if he hadn't also been such a talented artist, he might be remembered as a scientist who "sketched a little" on the side. Leonardo was uniquely placed historically, bridging the gap between the hocus-pocus of the Medieval period, and inquiries of "modern" science. At the end of the Dark Ages in the fifteenth century, the scientific discoveries of classical Rome and Greece had been largely abandoned in favor of biblical teachings, which were taken as literal truth by most of the population.

Leonardo broke with this tradition by actually asking questions, and from his earliest days, he made detailed observations of the natural world around him. This work soon led to a desire to understand and predict, rather than just describe. Leonardo's tenacity and his varied interests allowed him to make important observations and discoveries in a wide range of scientific fields, from anatomy to zoology. His studies of the motion and the behavior of fluids (such as water) were impressive. He investigated plants, animals, and geology. In addition, Leonardo made notes on astronomical topics, such as the nature of the moon, sun, and stars, and fossil formation.

Although Leonardo's observation-based method seems simple to us today, his technique was revolutionary in his day. He would ask a seemingly simple question, such as "How do birds fly?" and then spend weeks or months making painstaking observations. These observations would include watching birds in flight, sketching birds in various poses, observing live birds close-up, and dissecting birds to understand their musculature and anatomy. He then translated his notes into a more general theoretical understanding of aerodynamics and flight. Leonardo, being the hands-on guy that he was, then designed flying machines that would give humans the same experience as birds.

Leonardo also pioneered the technique of scientific illustration. While we take for granted the technical drawings that appear in our textbooks, we really should thank Leonardo for coming up with this idea. He filled many of his notebooks with meticulous sketches, accompanied by detailed notes, of various anatomical or mechanical principles. Unlike his predecessors, who relied on long-winded explanations, Leonardo felt that his sketches and drawings were the primary tool in illustrating his various points; his written notes were actually secondary. Sometimes a picture really is worth a thousand words!

Love that body!

Leonardo da Vinci was a man who could appreciate a great body. And all in the interest of science, really! During his lifetime, the field of medicine was becoming more important, and artists were increasingly fascinated with drawing the human body accurately. In Leonardo's case, he went a step further to figure out how the bodily systems beneath the surface worked. Leonardo's early paintings were studies in a new humanistic style of art, and he was way ahead of his contemporaries in this regard. The best example is his *Vitruvian Man* drawing of 1490, one of the first accurate expressions of the relationship between the human form and geometrical proportions. Leonardo's interest in anatomy ran deep, both literally and figuratively. He spent years researching the intricacies of how our bodies function. In 1489, he started work on a notebook focused specifically on anatomy. He studied all parts of the body, especially the brain and eyes. He sketched skulls in cross-section, showing both an amazing understanding of the visible and an interpretive ability to figure out the unknown. His drawings demonstrate a clear relationship between eyes, nose, teeth, jaw, and vertebrae. To make things clearer, he detailed most sketches with notes and measurements—almost like an architect doing construction documents. Many of Leonardo's other sketches define human anatomy with an unprecedented degree of detail. His drawings of the human ribcage, spine, and coccyx are highly accurate. He also rendered sketches of nudes in various positions, indicating a significant understanding of how the human form worked in motion.

Also, as the doctors of the day were only starting to realize, the best way to truly learn about the inner workings of the human body was, simply, to take a look inside. In order to study musculature and bone structures in the arms, legs, and other body parts, Leonardo dissected corpses in the early 1500s, possibly including a homeless woman who had been about nine months pregnant at the time of her death. One of his sketches shows a human fetus, complete inside a woman's body with placenta and uterus. Leonardo's drawings describe a curled fetus and umbilical cord as they lay inside the womb. However, in his drawings the unborn baby is a highly muscular infant. From this error, we can see that his factual knowledge was probably minimal. Despite some mistakes, Leonardo was one of the first to draw the female reproductive system accurately, and his drawings are certainly the most detailed to come from the Renaissance period. He also drew detailed sketches of other systems and organs, including the human heart.

Leonardo's work, detailing the nature of organs that had been previously undefined, was quite daring for the time. Renaissance clergy and others were of the mindset that the heart was some sort of spiritual element, not just a muscle like any other in the body. Although Leonardo explored science in rational, realistic terms, he did not dismiss spiritual notions. He always acknowledged the divine in his scientific studies, marveling at the complex beauty God had created.

From the inside out: Studies of human systems

Leonardo never stopped trying to learn more about the human body. You might even call him art's first forensic scientist. Not content just to draw the body as he saw it from the outside, he strove to understand the human form from the inside. How far would he go to increase this understanding? Farther than was acceptable or even legal at that time. He cut up cadavers, studied organs and skeletal substructures—all in an effort to draw and paint more accurately. Circulation and musculature systems intrigued him for the same reason. But what mattered most to Leonardo was the quality of his work, and he was willing to get his hands dirty—literally—to ensure that quality.

It wasn't just the body itself that interested Leonardo; he plunged deeper inside to study blood circulation and the heart, first in the 1490s, and again about twenty years later when he produced many drawings that detailed human circulation. Leonardo never figured out the exact connection between blood flow and the heart muscle, though. He used his studies of animals (and later, humans) to map out the basics: The heart was a four-chambered muscle somehow connected to the pulse you could feel in your wrist. Leonardo also figured out that arteries could become overfilled and that this situation could lead to sickness or even death. And so he actually predicted the concept of clogged arteries—an ailment that would become a major medical focus in later centuries.

Leonardo also paid particular attention to musculature, as we can see in several of his sketches. Some of his earlier anatomical drawings show extremely muscular men (perhaps indicating his own preferences), while later sketches focus more on anatomical detail. A series of shoulder drawings from 1511 show tremendous schematic detail on the layering of bodies, depicting skin, bone, muscle, and surrounding tissue as a complex web. Leonardo's paintings from twenty years earlier show this same fascination with the muscle groups, which create sculpted definition.

And now on to the fun stuff—sex! Leonardo was very interested in human reproduction. He initially thought the male reproductive organs had a direct channel that went straight to the heart and lungs and, therefore, the brain. (Hippocrates, a Greek physician from the fifth century B.C. and one of the founders of modern medicine, originally suggested these views.) As mentioned earlier in reference to the heart (see number 48), the popular view during the Renaissance was that bodily organs represented divine, spiritual entities. In keeping with this tradition, Leonardo considered the main outputs of the male sex organs as, essentially, sperm and "spirit." He also believed the human heart was a spirit. Nice idea, but he quickly realized that this approach was wrong because it could not be proven. The idea of a "spiritual channel" could simply not be borne out by the cold, hard evidence that Leonardo personally witnessed. At least Leonardo was willing to admit when he made a mistake—wouldn't it be nice if everyone did?

Fawning over flora

Leonardo began his long history of drawing animals by studying them in nature. Many of his paintings show different animals, some moving and some standing still. *The Adoration of the Magi*, for example, includes horses, a camel, and a mysterious third creature that Leonardo never finished. He also sketched an iconographically significant lamb in *The Virgin and Child with Saint Anne* (see number 39), though he himself may not have painted that particular portion of the work.

The horse was one of Leonardo's favorite animals. We know about his obsession with them because they're the animal he sketched the most. He drew them standing, sleeping, and in various states of motion. His *Statue of Francesco Sforza* (see number 29), if completed, would have been the largest monument of a horse anywhere in Europe. Toward the end of his life, Leonardo also made many bronze horse models that he gave to his final patron, King François I.

Leonardo's notebooks also prominently feature cats. He wrote stories about cats and sketched them in precise detail. He drew felines in a variety of positions, both asleep and in motion. Leonardo gave a cat the central focus in at least one of his paintings, *The Madonna with the Cat*. Leonardo also painted other animals at different points throughout his career, including pigs, bears, goats, birds, and dragons. There are also drawings of several animals that look like either crossbreeds or completely fictional beasts.

What is unique about Leonardo's drawings of animals is that he applied the same principles of geometry and proportion to them as he did to his architectural drawings. He made notes, for example, about how a horse's ear should be one-fourth as long as its face. He also studied the movement of birds in flocks and tried to rationalize their tendency to fly in circles. When he wanted to paint animals as accurately as possible, Leonardo knew that he would have to learn more about how their bodies functioned. His notebooks tell us that he made several visits to slaughterhouses. His sketches contain studies of dissected animals, including some highly detailed drawings of pig hearts. Once he revealed the animal's innards, Leonardo was able to see the still-beating heart and observe how blood was moving out of the heart and through the arteries. These scientific sketches were extremely significant because they were the first of their kind. Not only artists, but also future doctors would study Leonardo's drawings and methods as they later began their own research into anatomy.

Leonardo's interest in the natural world spread to flora as well as fauna. Unfortunately, Leonardo's plant sketches are some of the worst preserved of any of his drawings. We do know he drew lots of plants because his first biographer, Giorgio Vasari (1511–1574), tells us so. One existing sketch is the *Star of Bethlehem*, which was created between 1505 and 1507. This sketch is significant because, in addition to being one of his few surviving plant drawings, it shows a highly stylized, abstract flower. In contrast, most of his earlier plant drawings were more scientifically accurate. While a single flower may not seem like such a big deal, it's important to understand that Leonardo didn't just paint what he saw—he was also very creative.

Other surviving drawings include mountainous landscapes and rivers. Leonardo made these artworks in media such as metalpoint, chalk, and pen and ink. He is also known for the detailed botanical renderings of various plants and trees that exist in some of his paintings. While many Renaissance artists focused exclusively on the painting's central figure, Leonardo paid attention to every detail, and his work is richer because of it.

51

The perfect man

One of the most famous drawings of all time is Leonardo da Vinci's *Vitruvian Man* of 1490 (see the cover of this book). In the original sketch, which currently resides in Venice, Leonardo used both ink and watercolor. Leonardo's image has become an icon for art, science, and the Renaissance. Today it's such a widely recognized symbol, you can see it everywhere—in high-school textbooks and museum galleries, even on T-shirts. What is it about this particular drawing that has generated such attention? What is this drawing even about?

The source of inspiration for the *Vitruvian Man* was, not surprisingly, Vitruvius. But who was he? He was actually a Roman engineer from the first century B.C. who codified some of the first basic principles of architecture. Serving as chief architect under Julius Caesar, Vitruvius was ancient Rome's resident expert in urban planning and structural design, and he wrote the first definitive treatise on architecture, *The Ten Books on Architecture* (around 27 B.C.), in which he specified guidelines for city planning, building materials, hydraulics, and other civic projects. This influential book also established differences for religious, private, and public designs—the first time that such distinctions had been laid out so clearly. In addition to providing rules and principles for architects to follow, Vitruvius expressed the important relationship between architecture and social-cultural values.

It is likely that Leonardo's first exposure to Vitruvius, and his ideas on form and proportion, came during his apprenticeship to Verrochio. He was also probably influenced by Alberti's interpretations of the same subject. But Leonardo, as usual, came up with his own radical uses and interpretations.

In fact, Leonardo's *Vitruvian Man* could have been a poster child for Renaissance ideals of humanism and proportion. The drawing consists of a square that is partially inscribed in a circle, with a human male form inscribed into the combination of these two basic geometric shapes. This drawing has become so celebrated because it's the first example of a human form that wasn't forced into an unnatural distortion simply to accommodate the geometry.

Architecture, for Leonardo and most Renaissance architects, was a matter of harmonious modularity. As Leonardo proved with this drawing, it was possible to view the human body the same way: a composition of anatomical building blocks comparable to those of the built world. Interestingly, it's been said that in a not-so-rare moment of artistic hubris, Leonardo may have borrowed his own self-portrait to use for the head of Vitruvius in this influential work! Doesn't it seem appropriate, though, that Leonardo himself might be both model and artist for this symbol of the Renaissance?

Getting physical with science

Leonardo did more than draw circles and squares! Sure, he studied anatomy, but his interest in science didn't end there. He was also a student of the physical and natural sciences. In particular, he used his methods of observation and inquiry to look at a number of problems in physics, geology, astronomy, and other fields.

In geology, Leonardo's contribution is particularly striking. While working as part of Duke Sforza's court, Leonardo devoted time to surveying various mountains and valleys, and this work served as background for military engineering projects, such as making roads and tunnels. During this period, Leonardo most likely had ample time to study the area's various rocks, and he also observed the fossils (mostly mollusk shells) present within the rocks. From his writings, we know that Leonardo understood the process of sedimentary rock formation, which occurs through sequential deposition of small layers in a watery environment. He also understood erosion, the idea that wind, rain, and rivers progressively wear away rocks. In fact, he realized that, as a result of erosion, sand and rock particles are eventually carried to the ocean to repeat the cycle.

How is it that shells could be found in rocks that currently lay atop mountains? Scientists pondered this central geological question in Leonardo's day, and Leonardo rejected the two main suggestions prevalent at that time, which held that the shells had either been carried there by the great flood mentioned in the Bible, or that they had formed there in the rocks. From his observations of nature, Leonardo knew that shells had to come from living creatures and that these living creatures would have had to move around to eat and grow— they couldn't have formed inside a rock. He also noted that the world probably wasn't ever covered by a single great flood, since the water wouldn't have had anywhere to drain. Even if a flood had taken place locally in biblical times, any shells carried up to the mountaintops would have formed a jumbled mess, not the orderly layers that Leonardo saw.

Remarkably, Leonardo's solution to this puzzle came very close to the modern understanding. He suggested that when the fossils had been living sea creatures, they had been in an ocean environment. At some later time, mountains formed, and their gradual formation lifted the ocean sediments up to the mountain peaks. In fact, we know today that this model is a pretty good approximation of what actually happened!

But Leonardo didn't have the same good luck with all of his scientific theories; some of his beliefs were just wrong. In the field of astronomy, for example, Leonardo seemed to think that the sun and moon both orbited around the earth, and that the moon reflected the light of the sun because it was covered with water. Although he tried his best and did conduct some experiments with optics and lenses, telescopes were not invented until 100 years after Leonardo's time.

According to a sketch from 1510, Leonardo did manage to calculate a way to determine the distance from the earth to the moon, and the earth to the sun. He was also apparently one of the first to realize that even when only part of the moon was lit, the dark part of the crescent moon could still be seen faintly. (This illumination comes from sunlight that bounces off the earth and is then reflected off the moon.)

Clearly, while some of Leonardo's achievements in science were noteworthy, others weren't. Looking back, you could say that Leonardo's theoretical studies were generally less important than his practical innovations. However, you can also see that his inventions allowed Leonardo to discover and pursue new theoretical lines of research. Even modern scientists often need both theories and experiments to make breakthroughs!

It's all in the circle game

Leonardo first became interested in geometry while he was working for Duke Sforza in the 1480s and 1490s. He first encountered mathematical constructs— geometry in particular—through his study of architecture and perspective painting. In 1496, the well-known mathematician Luca Pacioli was invited to Sforza's court, nominally to teach mathematics there, and Leonardo and Pacioli became friends in Milan, apparently spending much time together discussing the overlap between art and mathematics. During his time in Milan, Pacioli was writing a book, later published as the first of a three-volume set in 1509, called *Divina Proportione*. Leonardo was so interested in this project that he actually drew the figures for this text.

Leonardo's drawings of three-dimensional shapes called polyhedra (one example is a soccer ball) were the highlight of Pacioli's book. Leonardo came up with a new way of drawing these complicated shapes—he showed them with solid edges and hollow faces that let you see right through them to the structure on the other side. For the book, Leonardo drew about sixty pairs of illustrations. Each pair showed a different three-dimensional shape, in both a solid view and a hollow view. Some of the shapes were new—no one had figured out how to draw them before!

The method of drawing shapes was a breakthrough for the day, and it took a visual artist of Leonardo's talents to come up with it. Leonardo's obsession with geometry continued even after he finished working on Pacioli's book. If you look through his notebooks, you'll find sketches of different geometric shapes in unlikely places, for example, among studies for military fortifications and designs for a fountain.

In addition to his direct work with Pacioli, Leonardo spent some time in Milan conducting his own research into geometry based on that of Euclid and Pacioli. In particular, he was interested in trying to "square a circle," meaning he wanted to find a way of creating a square with the same area as a particular circle, using only drawing tools such as a ruler and compass.

Beyond his theoretical work in mathematics, Leonardo was also interested in the mechanical methods of automating mathematical work, and he designed a machine that could have been one of the first calculators. A working replica was built in 1968, but whether or not this replica actually represented Leonardo's intention is another story. The sketches on which the calculating machine replica was based are unclear, and it's possible that the machine was not, in fact, a calculating machine, but a ratio machine instead.

Before planes, trains, and automobiles

Renaissance inventors were at a crossroads, whether they knew it or not. Europe was slowly emerging from the Dark Ages, and there had already been several significant inventions. At the same time, some of history's greatest achievements were yet to come. Leonardo, living fairly early in the Renaissance period, was on the leading edge of the era's innovation. Against what backdrop can we view his inventions?

One of the most significant inventions of the Renaissance was the mechanical timepiece. Though Casio calculator wristwatches wouldn't come along for a while yet, society was beginning to place more importance on an easy way to tell the time. Clocks were first created in the 1300s, but it was not until the 1580s that Galileo (a scientist and researcher from Florence) developed the idea for a pendulum. It wasn't until the 1600s, long after Leonardo's death, that the concept of the clock was further mechanized with the introduction of gears and screws.

Certainly, Leonardo and his contemporaries didn't have access to most of the modern conveniences we take for granted today. One of the things most noticeably lacking was electricity, which was not discovered until the seventeenth century and not widely used until the late 1800s. The first standardized fuel type was probably fish oil used by ancient Romans and those who came after them, so in the absence of electric lighting, fuel-driven lanterns would have been a possibility for Leonardo. Candles, torches, and lamps were other popular light sources during the Renaissance years.

In terms of weaponry, Leonardo had the advantage of *not* starting from scratch. Military technology, even in ancient Rome, was years ahead of the general technology available to the rest of the population. Hand-powered weapons such as spears and arrows had been around for generations, and gunpowder was in use by the middle of the eleventh century, though it probably wasn't used in Europe until the 1350s. This invention changed the course of warfare because it became nearly impossible to defend against guns with only hand-powered weapons. Leonardo's designs for cannons, for example, were a response to the new way of waging war.

Eyeglasses were another significant Medieval and Renaissance invention. By the 1300s, guilds in Venice were regulating eyeglass production, which, at the time, were probably considered a luxury item. When Johannes Gutenberg's invention of the printing press (see number 61) made reading into more of a hobby than a luxury, though, eyeglasses came into much higher demand. Everyone wanted to read, and their eyes needed to keep up with them! Readily available books were a major factor for Leonardo because he was able to read the writings of ancient masters and, in the process, create his own interpretations and additions. Plus, if books could be published easily, he could also publish his own writings. In addition to all of these other inventions, Leonardo used the growing worldwide interest in mechanics to utilize and explore water. Naturally, his concepts relied on existing research with water pumps, which were developed in the Middle Ages.

War games

When several Florentine forts were attacked in 1479, Leonardo became interested in ladders for scaling walls during an attack as well as methods for defending against those same efforts. Military engineering was just one of Leonardo's many interests, but as with everything else, he dove into it wholeheartedly and came up with several important designs.

Leonardo designed a number of different ladders for wall climbing. Some were stiff, solid ladders, while others were flexible and made from rope. To attach securely to the top of the wall, some of Leonardo's ladders had hooks; others had spikes on the base to keep them immobile on the ground. He also thought about flexible ladders that could hang from a wall as well as the type of chain ladder that's often used for fire escapes today. Ladders were, in a way, a symptom of the problem: war. Leonardo got to the root of the issue and also designed entire defense systems. One of his most clever ideas involved ladders lining a wall, where the tops of the ladders were all attached to a bar. Leonardo's assumption was that attackers would rush to climb the ladders in a sneak attempt to overtake the castle inside. Not so fast! Leonardo's defensive soldiers would push the bar out, and any poor, unsuspecting attackers would fall to the ground along with the row of ladders. It sounds complicated, and it was; perhaps this overdesign was one of the reasons it was never tested.

During his time with Duke Sforza, Leonardo also designed bridges for military applications. Some of these were portable; troops could carry the bridges with them and set them up quickly when needed. Others were designed to be particularly strong and resistant to fire or other means of destruction. Leonardo also considered methods to burn and destroy enemy bridges.

Leonardo's military bridges had a number of different designs. One was arched in such a way as to be particularly strong when assembled. Others used traditional pilings, or were flexible so they could swing without breaking. Leonardo also designed adjustable jacks for opposite sides of a river, to be used if the banks were different heights on each side.

Leonardo designed one particularly massive bridge during his time with Cesare Borgia. In order to connect the Golden Horn and the Bosporus, Leonardo suggested building a huge bridge across the Gulf of Istanbul. This route would have had immense strategic importance, but other engineers vetoed the plan when they saw how large the bridge would have to be. Nevertheless, modern studies show that the structure would have been possible to build with the resources of that era, and the bridge itself would have been solid and well designed.

Vehicles that could serve offensive or defensive purposes also piqued Leonardo's design curiosity. Take, for instance, his design for a horse-drawn chariot, which had four large scythe-like blades mounted to the axles. As the horse pulled the chariot, the blades would rotate, slicing off the limbs of enemy soldiers. A similar design placed the four large blades at the front of the machine, in front of the horses even, where a screw-type device turned them, and included a series of smaller scythe blades placed at the back of the chariot. This chariot was designed as a brutal weapon, indeed. Even the initial sketches included images of dead and dying soldiers left in its wake. For the peace-loving Leonardo, this was an incredibly gruesome design!

56

Building a better . . . cannon?

Leonardo's peaceful, harmonious landscape paintings do not tell the entire story of his career. In addition to his work to support troops with better ladders and bridges, Leonardo also designed or improved weapons. Guns, cannons, and other artillery weapons were on the rise during the Renaissance. Newer was better, especially when it came to national defense. Leonardo appeared to have had a nostalgic side, though, because he still spent time working to perfect or improve older weapons such as catapults, slingshots, and crossbows.

One of his innovations was the rapid-firing crossbow. This was no ordinary crossbow—it actually included four crossbows and got its power from a large treadmill. A number of men walked on steps that were located around the outside of a large wheel, and as they made the machine rotate, an archer would fire each crossbow, reloading them in sequence.

Leonardo also designed a mammoth seventy-six-foot crossbow, which required six wheels to maneuver it. This device, also called a ballista, used a series of gears to draw back the bow; a simple strike of a pin would release the shaft. Leonardo believed that this giant weapon would operate in almost complete silence, but his claim was never tested because the device was too difficult to build given the abilities of the day.

In the interest of defeating more enemies faster, Leonardo designed a rapid-loading catapult system. This machine, which could be mounted on top of a wall, consisted of a rope and winding mechanism used to bend back the arm and, in effect, ease the firing process. Leonardo also designed a row of catapults that could be launched at the same time when hit with hammers. Specially designed missiles, with gunpowder inside, had fins on the tail for extra stability, and when they hit their target, strikers inside ignited the gunpowder and caused an explosion. These sound remarkably similar to modern artillery shells.

While cannons were used as early as 1346, they weren't very advanced by Leonardo's time. They were still simple cylinders that used an explosion of gunpowder at one end to propel a stone ball out the other. One of Leonardo's first improvements to cannon design was to create a model that could be loaded from the back, rather than down the front of the barrel. Since the cannons had to be cooled before they could be reloaded, Leonardo suggested putting them in a vat of water to cool them off quickly. Not a bad idea, but would *you* want to be the one to lift a hot cannon into a tub?

In his studies of cannon balls, Leonardo was one of the first to explore ballistic trajectories. He studied how changing the angle of the cannon's muzzle could affect the distance the cannonball traveled, and in testing his designs, he supposedly launched a test cannonball 10,000 feet high!

Another invention of Leonardo's was a steam-powered cannon. The end of the cannon was heated to a very high temperature, and then a small amount of water was placed inside. As the water turned to steam, the increased pressure shot out the speeding cannonball. Leonardo's notebooks include information on the size of cannonballs that the device could use, and the distance they could travel. These details suggest that, unlike most of his inventions, this one was actually built and tested.

One problem that plagued Leonardo was that cannons had a large delay between repeated firings. Leonardo's answer was, in retrospect, pretty obvious: He proposed a system with multiple cannons that could either be fired all at once, or one after another. His designs included eleven or fourteen guns in three rows: While the top row was being fired, the middle row could be reloaded, and the bottom row cooled off. These systems are considered to be the predecessors of today's machine guns. Just think about how dangerous Leonardo would be today if he were making improvements to modern military technology!

Leonardo's robot

Compared to, say, the history of architecture, the field of robotics is relatively new. Most development in this area has happened in the twentieth century. However, leave it to Leonardo to be at the front of the pack! He was one of the first to have an impact on robotics design.

In 1495, Leonardo sketched out an idea for a mechanical robot that may have been the first such design in history. It was a mechanical, humanlike figure whose purpose was somewhat unclear—maybe Leonardo designed it just for fun! Leonardo's robot could turn its head via a bendable neck, open and close its jaw (which was close to being anatomically correct), move its arms, and sit up and down. In the drawing, the robot looks like a knight, since it appears to be wearing a suit of armor. It was designed with at least two gear systems that operated separately from each other: one to control the lower body (legs, feet, hips) and one for the upper body (arms, shoulders, hands).

You could call this robot design a culmination of Leonardo's research into anatomy and geometry. What better way to combine mechanical science and human form? He took the proportions and relationships inherent in Roman architecture and applied them to the movement and life inherent in all living beings. In a way, the robot was *Vitruvian Man* brought to life.

Historians are not certain that a physical model of Leonardo's robot was ever constructed. This design was misplaced for many years and was only discovered in the 1950s. Computer models of Leonardo's design have since been constructed, attempting to show how his robot might have been realized in sixteenth-century Italy.

58

Chutes (we already covered ladders)

Leonardo was a flyboy from day one. As a child, he spent hours watching birds. He drew every kind he saw, and this fascination stayed with him throughout his life. He was particularly interested in wings, and they occupy page after page of his notebooks. He did more than draw, though—he actually set out to make himself a pair of wings. The design matured into something resembling a modern parachute. Probably the first of its kind, this design depicted a fabric-based device that a person could use to float from the sky onto the ground.

His first parachute, seen in one of his early notebooks, probably dates to 1485. This design looks a lot like a modern kite, with a person dangling from an airborne fabric structure that was held together by rigid poles. The parachute itself would probably have been made of linen, sealed at the edges so it wouldn't unravel or fray during flight. The poles would have been arranged in a pyramidal shape, with a maximum length of about twenty feet. (In contrast, modern parachutes all use flexible structures and fabric.)

Unlike the parachutes of today, most of Leonardo's designs made no real provisions for personal safety. His notes suggest that the parachute could be used from any tall outcropping, and the user would be perfectly safe upon arrival back to earth:

> *"If a man had a tent made of linen, of which all the apertures have been stopped up, and it be twelve braccia [twenty-one feet] across and twelve feet in depth, he will be able to throw himself down from any great height without sustaining any injury."*

However, the rigid structure probably could have caused serious injury if it crumpled on top of the passenger inside. Like most of his other inventions, however, Leonardo's parachute was never built and tested during his lifetime. One of the biggest hurdles was probably finding something high enough to jump from!

Leonardo's design was finally tested in June of 2000 by a skydiver and camera flyer named Adrian Nicholas. After constructing a version of Leonardo's design using canvas, wooden poles, and ropes, Nicholas landed safely after jumping from a hot air balloon at 10,000 feet (for safety reasons, he broke out a modern frameless parachute 2,000 feet from the ground). Leonardo's parachute actually floated to the ground more slowly than a traditional parachute would have. While most people thought that Leonardo's design wouldn't work or would spin too much to keep the occupant from excessive nausea, Nicholas proved that the master's design was flight worthy. A model of Leonardo's parachute currently hangs in the British Library in London.

It's a bird, it's a plane, it's a flying machine!

Leonardo's first memory, as he tells it in his notebooks, was of himself as a small baby, lying in a cradle outside, minding his own business, when a hawklike bird called a kite landed on him and poked its tail feathers in his mouth. While it would have been extremely unusual for an infant to retain such a memory (as well as unlikely that such a bird would even land on a baby), it might explain Leonardo's later obsession with flight!

Leonardo started with the assumption that people could eventually fly using their own strength, and he tried to design a device to help them do just that. He also wrote up his ideas about flight into a treatise now called the *Codex on the Flight of Birds*. In these notes, he summarized his scientific theories about how birds were actually able to fly, including his idea that the wing's movement created circular areas of wind thrust. Not so shabby for a fifteenth-century scientist!

In the course of his studies, Leonardo determined that human-powered aircraft would be difficult to build and use. In the late 1480s, he repeatedly studied an ornithopter, an aircraft that was almost completely powered by flapping wings. He wanted to create a machine that would mimic the flight of a bird as much as possible. Other designers after Leonardo continued research in this area, although it was never very popular once aircrafts with other means of propulsion came along.

Unfortunately, Leonardo's initial flapping-wing designs required balance, coordination, and strength. Even Da Vinci realized this would be too much to expect from most people! For that reason, Leonardo also focused on simpler designs. One of these was for a glider system with birdlike wings. In this device, which must have been inspired by a bat or other small winged creature, the user would climb in, jump off a mountain or tall tree, and balance primarily by moving the lower body in conjunction with the wings. Leonardo created another version of the design where the "pilots" moved their legs up and down, and another one in which a spring-loaded mechanism did most of the work.

Leonardo spent a lot of time working on the flapping system mechanism. Unfortunately for him, he paid little attention to the role feathers play in flight. This turned out to be one of his greatest oversights! Plus, as his flying machines got more complicated, they also got heavier and heavier—and therefore less likely to actually succeed. Aeronautical engineering in the fifteenth century was virtually nonexistent, so history can easily forgive Leonardo's technological mistakes.

Of all his flying machines, the sketches for Leonardo's glider are particularly interesting because he laid out the drawings in plan, section, and elevation on a single sheet. This degree of precision indicates he probably intended to build a scale model. Toward the end of his life, Leonardo focused primarily on fixed-wing craft, such as gliders, that relied more heavily on the concept of lift than on the physical act of flapping. These, at least, had some hope of actually getting off the ground some day!

The "Codex Atlanticus," one of Leonardo's notebooks, contains many designs and notes on machines. It includes descriptions of flight patterns he observed in birds and displays several designs for aircraft with movable wings. He also mentions test flights that may actually have been conducted from Mount Ceceri—supposedly a student of his broke a leg while conducting such a flight! Unlike most of Leonardo's inventions, which were never built, Leonardo (or his unwitting students) tested at least a few of his designs for flying machines. How successful they were, though, is another story.

60

Leonardo's whirlybird

Why limit yourself to "traditional" flying machines? In addition to parachutes, gliders, bat wings, and other assorted fliers, Leonardo created some of the world's first helicopter designs. While he borrowed the form from some of his previous designs, he created something radically different in terms of structure and mechanics.

Leonardo's helicopter design used a corkscrew-shaped propeller instead of the blades seen on modern helicopters. The occupants rode in a basket that would have been made of wooden poles, with their feet planted on a platform that ended shortly before the screw-shaped blade began. Leonardo's idea, according to his notes, was to use a spring-loaded system that would wind up the helicopter and then release it. He used this idea again in his design for a car (see number 67). If this screw spun fast enough, he hypothesized, the entire machine would rise from the ground. What's unclear is whether or not the occupants would have been spinning along with the blade! The very idea is enough to give most people motion sickness, so it's probably good that he didn't make anyone test it out during his lifetime.

The major problem with Leonardo's design was its weight. It simply would have been too heavy to lift off the ground. In addition, while his idea of the human-powered machine was decidedly humanistic in concept, the reality was that no person would be able to generate enough power to actually take his helicopter up into the air. Leonardo gave the typical man (and woman) way too much credit in this case.

After many years of failed designs, Leonardo's dream came to fruition when Igor Sikorsky, a Russian aviator and inventor, studied Da Vinci's sketches and notes and, in 1910, began drawing prototypes for a working helicopter. Leonardo would have been proud—and probably would have taken the first test flight.

The world before Xerox

The responsibility of reproducing written works prior to the fifteenth century fell to monks, who were both literate and skilled in the art of transcription. Their task was not an easy one; they had to copy each word and illustration by hand from one piece of paper to another. Without even getting into the terrible inefficiency, there were several obvious problems with this method. The monks made lots of mistakes, and they were hard to fix. With each copy all the illustrations had to be completely redrawn, and it's unlikely that the transcription monks were artists of Leonardo's caliber. Say hello to stick figures! It probably wasn't *that* bad, but there was also little point in reproducing a book of drawings. In addition, the paper used most often in the pre-Renaissance era was parchment made from animal skin, and like most things of natural origin, it simply didn't last forever. The fact that each and every book had to be made by hand created very high costs, making literature unaffordable for most people.

Things began to change in 1446 when Johannes Gutenberg came roaring into the world of reproduction, creating the first printing press and altering the courses of literature, education, and society at large. It's impossible to overstate the importance of the printing press. Gutenberg combined movable type (previously invented in China) with ink, brass plates, and paper to create an array. Letters could be formed into words, and the results could be printed.

The outcome of the printing press was immediate and immense. All of a sudden, people could afford to buy books. Kids had no excuse not to go to school! Many more people learned to read and write, and society had to keep up with this influx of newly educated workers. The fun didn't stop with books—both text and music could be printed, and more and more people wanted sheet music. And don't forget about the papermaking industry—it developed new methods for creating paper more quickly, cheaply, and efficiently. There was money to be made here, and everyone wanted a share.

The ability to reprint ancient treatises and documents also factored in to the aims of the Renaissance—the classics could be brought to life. People could read Vitruvius, Aristotle, and other ancient Greeks and Romans. In addition, wealthier people who already had access to books started requesting a greater variety of literature, in different languages. There was suddenly a demand for poetry! Almanacs! Many new types of books were created, and they quickly became popular.

Always true to form, Leonardo approached the printing press critically. The predecessor to the printing press was block printing, a method where a block of wood would be carved out to leave raised letters. In Gutenberg's updated printing press model, letters (type) were placed by hand along a track, and these letters were movable, meaning they could be reset for each new page of text. While Leonardo didn't propose completely reinventing the printing press, he had an idea to add a second track that would increase the machine's efficiency. He wanted to publish a treatise on this idea, but like most of his works, it remained undiscovered until well after his death.

The printing press had immense ramifications for Leonardo's future work. And everyone—future artists, inventors, school children—has benefited from being able to read the master's original work.

Under the boardwalk, down by the sea

Leonardo was a considerate soul. Not only was he interested in the design of boats and other watercraft, he also thought about the needs of sailors themselves. One thing we can't credit Leonardo with, though, is inventing diving. The ancient Greeks used a technique called breath-hold diving to search for food, gather sponges, and perform military reconnaissance. The Greeks and Romans swam underwater to escape enemy detection, probably by breathing through reeds. Some people supposedly experimented with breathing from an air-filled bag underwater, but the recycled carbon dioxide likely put an end to those trials.

Swimming, diving, and generally working with water were ideas Leonardo pursued constantly. He tried to expand the length of time someone could stay underwater, and he also wanted to find ways to protect the submerged diver. Aside from dangerous fish, there were underwater plants to brush against, sharp rocks to step on, and too many other obstacles. Many of Leonardo's oceanic inventions were never tested, but some are quite similar to actual devices that can be purchased today.

One of his most futuristic ideas was a full deep-sea diving suit. Preliminary research into deep-sea exploration was beginning to take hold in the Renaissance, and Leonardo's ideas were influenced by this new interest in visiting the ocean depths. As with most things of a technological nature, the primary impetus (and, in most cases, funding) was likely the military. Italians had to become smarter about their battles, and water approaches were one way to take advantage of the natural terrain.

Leonardo's sketches show divers who were basically frogmen, prepared for land and sea at the same time. Their diving suits included land requirements such as regular clothes, ropes, and weapons. He also sketched out an "air sack" that may have sparked later inventors to create oxygen tanks. One such diagram shows the diver with a large, impact-resistant air tank attached to his chest so that he could dive far beneath the surface, but this chamber was so bulky, swimming with it might have been impossible! Leonardo's suit was to be made of leather or other durable animal skin, and cane hoses allowed the diver to move and breathe easily. He tried to reinforce these connections with metal, so that the pressure of being deep underwater wouldn't threaten the diver's safety. It seems Leonardo intended this suit for relatively shallow diving, because the pipe providing air to the diver went directly to the surface. The top of the tube also featured a bell-shaped float, so that the air openings would always remain above water. Modern divers have actually built a suit from Leonardo's notes, and they reported that it functioned quite well.

In true biblical spirit, Leonardo developed ideas in 1480 to let humans walk on water. Unlike Jesus, though, Leonardo's water walkers had to use special floating devices to keep them from sinking. This addition probably kept Leonardo from being deemed a heretic, and also added a touch of practicality, if you can call it that. These floats would have been attached to the feet of the user, who would have balanced by holding on to long poles. Not surprisingly, Leonardo doesn't seem to have ever built or tested a real version of this device.

Many of Leonardo's sketches for water-based machines focused on convenience. For example, he designed a glove with webbing in between the fingers, imitating a duck's webbed feet. These gloves would have been worn in the water, creating smoother and faster self-powered transportation. They also would have spared the wearer's hands from sticks, stinging fish, and other hazards. One of his sketches shows gloves proportionally as large as the flippers that swimmers wear on their feet! He also designed a life preserver that would allow people to remain afloat while in the water. While some of his inventions seem outlandish, others were practical and useful—the dreamer definitely had his pragmatic side.

Containing the forces of nature

Water: the basis for all life on earth, the universal solvent, and a general requirement for all living things. It has fascinated humans throughout recorded history, and Leonardo was no exception. He went to great depths to study water and all its properties. His observations were right on target. For example, he noted that water could easily change in character depending on the environment. Leonardo studied the various ways in which water came from the heavens, noting it could fall as rain, melt as snow, run in rivers, and actually come from the earth itself. He understood water's power to revitalize plants and people, but he was also aware of its ferociousness, as we can tell from his studies of storms and his sketches of powerful swirling waves.

Like his interest in blood flow and circulation, Leonardo was interested in river flow and water motion. As an artist he was always in motion, so you can definitely see the correlation. He studied currents and waves, observing how surfaces that repeatedly came into contact tended to degrade over time. He may have actually been the first to suggest the concept of erosion, and realizing how destructive water can be, he probably even feared the disaster caused by swollen rivers. As it turns out, his concern was well founded. The Arno River, near Florence and Pisa, erupted over its banks at least twice during Leonardo's lifetime, once in 1466 and again in 1478. These cataclysmic events influenced Leonardo's water management and manipulation designs.

One of his grandest ideas to control water was a scheme to divert the actual path of the Arno River. Leonardo was in Imola in 1502, working as the chief engineer for Cesare Borgia. During this time he used his skills in cartography to accurately plot out the course of the river, and in 1503 he presented a plan to redirect the river between Imola, Florence, and the sea. He had the support of influential Renaissance politician and philosopher Niccolò Machiavelli. Leonardo and Machiavelli were two of the most respected figures of the day, and their positions lent significant authority to their scheme.

At one point, Leonardo also decided to revamp the Florentine canal system. The general goal was to construct a series of channels that, passing through Pisa, would eventually lead to the sea. This effort would have improved the city's waterpower and irrigation, in addition to the commercial benefits. These canals would have used steps and locks powered by oversized siphons. In his engineering studies, Leonardo suggested digging large ditches that would eventually connect to the river. Ships could have sailed through Florence and into the hillier, mountainous areas for easier pickup and delivery of goods. It also would have helped with the Florentine wartime effort.

Unlike many of Leonardo's projects, this one was at least started! Hundreds of men began working on the canals under the supervision of Colombino, a master hydraulic engineer. Unfortunately, these canals were never completed, as Leonardo had to return to Florence to work on a fresco in the Palazzo Vecchio. In Leonardo's absence, Colombino took a few liberties with the design and made some disastrous engineering changes. According to some reports, the Arno actually did flow into its new path for a short time, but the river promptly reverted to its previous course and the project was eventually abandoned.

64

Harnessing the power of water

On dry land, Leonardo spent time studying and designing aircraft, including elaborate helicopters, gliders, and parachutes. Never one to limit himself, he was also fascinated with aquatics and devoted years to designing machines that worked with water. Given the sheer amount of water surrounding Italy, he picked a great hobby. It is likely that he was first exposed to aquatic engineering while apprenticed to Verrocchio, who was, among other things, a hydraulics engineer.

Why this interest in aquatics? From his observations, Leonardo knew water was inherently contradictory. He described it as the *vetturale di nature* (vessel of nature). It's only fitting that such a force of nature would have intrigued Leonardo. Between about 1485 and 1490, Leonardo developed several schemes for machines that worked in water. One design was for a water pump that could drain an entire port! This pump would have been useful when pylons had to be driven into water, or when a building's foundation had to be built underwater. He also developed pumps that could remove water from a ship (or anyplace else) through a valve.

Leonardo's "Codex Atlanticus" contains many designs for water-controlling devices. For example, he came up with several ideas for sluice gates, or movable panels, that could drop down to divert the flow of a river or canal. He also made detailed three-dimensional sketches for dredges (machines that could clean the bottom of locks and canals), which used mooring ropes to wind up the dredge and force it along the shoreline to the next point.

Some of Leonardo's drawings show machines that use water to achieve another purpose. He sketched a hydraulic saw that used water to power the blade; this device could have been used for cutting logs and other large objects. He also worked on a design that improved the Archimedian screw, an ancient device used to pump water out of a well or uphill. This design was similar to both his helicopter studies and a later waterwheel design. Waterwheels, though developed years before the Renaissance, were of great interest because of their capacity to quickly replenish supplies (such as the local water tower) that could be exhausted during battle.

Leonardo also created a water clock, which set off an alarm based on the amount of water flowing from one container to another. At its most basic, the water clock consisted of a stone jar or other container from which water dripped.

A second vessel was filled at a continuous rate. As the volume of water increased, people could use markings inside the container to see how much time had passed. It might not have the cachet of an hourglass, but it apparently worked quite well if you didn't mind the sound of dripping water!

The ocean liners of the future

Being the all-around inventor that he was, Leonardo tried his hand at designing all sorts of vehicles. He sketched schematics for many types of land- and watercraft, including the world's first paddleboat. His three-dimensional pen-and-ink sketches dating to 1482 show a pointed hull—a smart design idea, since it increased speed and enhanced navigation. He thought that if a boat could be propelled with paddles mounted on a rotating cylinder, the boat could move faster and more smoothly than with oars. His sketches were highly detailed in some places; he specified gears, belts, and large cylinders connecting the entire assembly.

Hull designs for ships were not new—even Stone Age humans figured out how to carve out the inside of a tree and use it for a canoe. Leonardo added his own special flare by improving on existing hull designs in both shape and ergonomics. In addition to a single-hull design, Leonardo sketched out a double hull that would make the ship stronger and better able to ward off enemies. This idea has endured into modern times, double-hull steel ships being quite common. He also worked on ways to resurrect sunken ships, one of which involved attaching tanks filled with air to the sides of a ship. The idea was that after an attack, ships could simply use these tanks to float back to the surface.

Some of Leonardo's designs for watercraft weren't even meant for people. He knew that Italy was industrializing, and a major side effect was that goods had to be transported. He made some sketches showing a float for transporting building materials down a river. A dropped bottom provided space for either passengers or military personnel. Another revolutionary design was for a partial submarine, or semisubmersible. Though it was intended for battle, only a couple of people could fit inside it. Like modern submarines, it did have a tower leading to the surface, but the similarity ended there.

Leonardo was definitely a proponent of "think big!" One of his largest boat designs was for a war ship that served as a battering ram. Leonardo's drawings show an oversized rotating scythe, operated by a gear-based mechanism that raised and lowered it. Leonardo's attention to detail is evident in this design, which also includes shields for the oarsmen. Modern-day descendents from these battleships were built in the mid-nineteenth century, including the iron-clad giants such as the USS *Monitor*. This type of warship is largely obsolete now due to the emergence of more flexibly designed aircraft carriers.

Around and around we go

The wheel is perhaps the undisputed champion of inventions. It has influenced virtually every part of civilization, from politics and government, to housing and recreation. Wheels are used in almost all forms of transportation: cars, trains, airplanes, and anything else that needs to move along a firm surface. Imagine a modern commute without bicycles, cars, and buses. Wheels are central to manufacturing and mass production, and most of us couldn't earn a living without them.

Leonardo da Vinci used wheels in many of his designs. He was interested in ways to increase efficiency and safety by automating mechanical tasks. Automation allows people to do more of what people are good at—philosophy, art, and other creative activities machines just can't do. Using machines to make life easier interested Leonardo, and he included the wheel as a foundation in many of his designs. Lots of Leonardo's machines used the wheel-and-axle concept. When wheels were fixed to an axle, turning one wheel meant that a second wheel would also turn. Leonardo was also interested in reducing the effort it took to turn something—while a large force was necessary to turn the wheel, it resulted in a much smaller force required to turn the smaller axle. So by using only a small force near the axle, a larger motion could be created in the wheel itself. Mechanical details like these show that Leonardo was not only interested in how machines worked, he also wanted them to work as easily as possible for their human operators. How considerate of him!

Pulleys were also important to Leonardo's designs. At its simplest, a pulley is just a wheel with a cable going over it, and two weights at the ends of the cable. Moving one weight down makes the second weight on the other side of the pulley rise. You can even connect pulleys into teams, making it possible to use less force when lifting heavy objects.

Leonardo also used gears in most of his machine sketches. First developed by the ancient Greeks, a gear is a toothed wheel that is placed next to other gears. When the first gear turns, its motion, and the force that goes with it, is transferred to the second gear. This setup is useful because it lets smaller gears use larger forces. You can also put gears at ninety-degree angles to each other. Leonardo's design for an adding machine (see number 53), for example, contained an elaborate system of gears and cranks. Historians aren't exactly sure how this machine would have worked, but they think users could have done either calculations or ratios. Toothed gears, though, were essential to the design.

Leonardo used the wheel in other types of devices, such as an odometer. Much simpler than the odometer in your car, Leonardo's idea was just to measure distance. This design was interesting because it had a handle, almost like an old-fashioned lawnmower, that you could hold while you walked. As the wheel turned, it turned a sprocket, making one stone fall into a basket every time the wheel went around once. You could then figure out how far you had gone just by counting the stones! Perhaps this system was a bit more complicated than looking at the digital display on your car, but it probably would have worked quite well.

Leonardo came up with many other inventions that used wheels, including precursors to the automobile and bicycle. More information on these inventions is in number 67.

67

Gone with the Schwinn

While Leonardo sometimes designed machines that had no practical use, others were actually quite functional. He sketched mechanical assemblies with no direct purpose, but also worked on inventions with immediate human application. If you were to go to Leonardo's showroom today, you'd find items such as a bicycle, an automobile, and a mechanical loom!

Out of all his sketches, Leonardo's bicycles were some of his most advanced. The most famous of these, found during a restoration of the "Codex Atlanticus," shows a device with two wheels connected by a chain, plus a seat and handlebars. It probably would have been made of wood, including the wheels. It looks eerily like a modern bicycle, although its rigid frame would have made it very hard to steer! Just to give you a sense of how far ahead of the pack Leonardo really was, he designed this sketch in 1493 and the next official bicycle design didn't come until the 1860s!

Don't get too excited, though: There are some questions about the authenticity of Leonardo's bicycle sketches. The sketch had never been seen before its discovery in the 1960s, and some historians think that, based on the ink type, drawing style, and extreme similarity to modern cycles, monks in possession of Leonardo's notebooks may have added it. Of course, it's still possible that the drawing was just stuck in between the pages of the notebook for centuries.

While Leonardo designed several horse-drawn carriages, he also leapt into the future with sketches for a spring-driven vehicle, which could have been the forebearer of the modern automobile! One of Leonardo's drawings shows self-pro-pelling vehicles that used a wheeled platform and coiled springs attached to gears, which the user had to wind. This design is actually similar to those of early auto-mobiles in which drivers had to manually crank the car. The winding only took care of half the problem, though, since the driver also had to steer. Do you know anyone coordinated enough to sit, steer, stand, and wind at the same time? We can breathe a collective sigh of relief that Henry Ford didn't steal Leonardo's design.

In addition to the bicycle, Leonardo drew several mechanical looms around 1495. This weaving machine, very intricately detailed, was intended to be completely automatic. You can tell from his design that Leonardo paid a lot of attention to how traditional weavers performed operations by hand. He actually devised gears and other machinery to achieve the same results, combining dif-ferent actions into one that could be controlled by a single crankshaft.

Leonardo went all out on this design, considering it one of the most impor-tant of the day. In a not-so-rare glimpse of hubris, Leonardo mentioned in his notebooks that he thought the loom rivaled the recent ability to print using mov-able type. The National Museum of Science and Technology (in Milan, Italy) seems to agree; they built a full-scale reconstruction and found that it worked perfectly. While Leonardo did not supply dimensions in his original drawings, the museum staff determined the size of the machine, working backwards based on the dimensions of a finished piece of cloth. Like so many of his designs, it's truly a shame that his loom was never built during the Renaissance—imagine how the course of history, or at least fashion, might have changed!

A coach fit for a king

Besides his designs for the bicycle and automobile, Leonardo created drawings of other vehicles. As engineers rose to the challenge of making more advanced war machines, Leonardo also contributed significantly to this effort. Leonardo designed new weapons and entirely new weapons systems (see number 56) and also came up with ideas for many different land vehicles. Some of his ideas were quite practical, while others appear more inventive, like modern automotive "concept cars" that are cool to look at, but would never be practical on the highway.

One of his largest vehicular designs was for an armored tank. The idea behind the armored car was simple: Protect passengers while causing as much damage as possible. Leonardo didn't specify the powering mechanism, and his notes indicate that his tank could have been either hand-cranked (as with his automobile design) or drawn by horses. If hand powered, the cranks would have been connected to gears, which, in turn, connected to the main driving wheels. Clad in metal panels, like today's tanks, it would have had holes for guns to poke through. In the drawing, it looks like a combination of a turtle and an alien spaceship. Do you think this vehicle would have struck awe, or just confusion, in the enemy?

Leonardo also designed vehicles for civilian usage. As architectural technology developed, the construction trade had to keep up. Lifting heavy materials to increasing heights was a well-documented problem throughout the Medieval period (just think about all those cathedrals!), and Leonardo came up with several ideas to remedy the situation. He sketched a number of designs for cranes that could be used for quarrying. The crane would lift a stone block out of the ground, and then a mechanism would automatically release once the load was removed from the quarry pit. Leonardo also drew three-dimensional designs for cranes that pivoted on a platform, which would have been useful for constructing tall buildings. While there don't appear to have been any crane models built during Leonardo's lifetime, later engineers have built them from his specifications and found them to be nearly flawless.

Part 4

WRITING, DRAWING, AND MUSIC

While painting and sculpture were Leonardo's primary focus, he was practically Shakespearean in the volume of written work he left behind. His notebooks contain thousands of pages of writing and drawing, and like a photographer uses film, Leonardo used his notebooks to capture both fact and intent. He documented scientific experiments and casual thoughts on art and science, using both text and accompanying illustrations. On more than one occasion, Leonardo strove for fame (if not fortune) by organizing his thoughts for future publication. With the exception of *A Treatise on Painting*, however, little of his writing was published until modern times. His notes were willed to his student and companion Francesco Melzi, but their importance was not recognized after Melzi's death. The thousands of pages were already dispersed, and many lost altogether. What remains of Leonardo's writings and drawings has been gathered together into various "codices" over the years.

In addition to his writings and sketches, Leonardo produced many drawings, as we've seen. Some were studies for eventual paintings, while others were portraits or self-portraits. In addition to his artistic works, he composed fables and short stories probably meant to amuse royal courts. He was also an excellent musician, improving on the design of a number of instruments of the day. He played a variety of instruments and was known to sing well. Leonardo was practically a one-man Renaissance halftime show! If nothing else, he was certainly, in every sense of the phrase, a Renaissance man.

The Leonardo diaries

Notes were Leonardo's method of choice for recording his observations about the world around him. He began this habit when he was about thirty-seven and continued it for the rest of his life. They didn't have spiral binding in the Renaissance, nor could Leonardo hit up the local art supply store for a diary. Instead, he composed on loose pieces of paper of varying sizes. You can imagine Leonardo jotting down his latest inspirations on whatever pieces of scrap paper he had lying around—the Renaissance equivalent of cocktail napkins and envelope backs, perhaps? These notes reflect Leonardo's own spirit: Instead of being an orderly succession of thoughts, they appear more like an unedited outpouring of Leonardo's brilliance.

And that was fine—no one else had to read his private records, or so Leonardo intended. They were practically written in a new language, anyway. As mentioned previously, Leonardo wrote in Italian, but he wrote backwards, from right to left (perhaps because he was left-handed) and in a mirror fashion, where all the letters were backwards as well. He also invented his own shorthand, abbreviating and combining words, or in some cases dividing one word into two. And just to make matters more difficult, Leonardo also abstained from punctuation!

Due to the scattered nature of Leonardo's notes, individual pages of Leonardo's notes may deal with a diversity of topics. For example, a page that begins with an astronomical study of the motion of the earth can end with a discussion of the mixing of colors to create different shades (i.e., red + yellow = orange).

Similarly, a page on the structure of the human intestines might finish as a discussion of the relationships between art and poetry. Even pages that consider one main topic are often covered with sketches or doodles of unrelated subjects.

Fortunately, Leonardo's observations are mostly self-contained on a single page of his notes. Leonardo was careful to note if they continued to the back of the page or to a different page altogether. Aside from this care in continuation, however, there is almost no overall order or numbering to the pages—few are even dated or numbered at all.

Selections from Leonardo's first published work, *A Treatise on Painting*, appeared in a 1651 volume put out by a French publisher, and the work became extremely popular. Reprinted in six different languages, it would have definitely been on the Renaissance best-sellers list, if there were such a thing. However, this book wasn't actually based on Leonardo's original notes, but on copies that only had a few small parts of the original. The published versions didn't even use Leonardo's original order or try to combine ideas logically.

The next significant development with Leonardo's published works occurred in 1880, when a Da Vinci specialist named Jean Paul Richter, who was inspecting a Leonardo manuscript from a private collection, discovered a large fragment of the text from *A Treatise on Painting* in its original form. What a find! Richter continued his scavenger hunt throughout Europe, eventually discovering many parts of the work. Richter was able to create a new version that was very close to resembling Leonardo's actual intentions. This "new" treatise includes many drawings and sketches to illustrate various points, and discusses perspective, light and shadow, color theory, the proportions of the human figure, as well as botany and landscape painting.

In addition to his notes on painting (the best developed of his notes and clearly destined for publication) Leonardo also wrote about other artistic topics. For instance, Leonardo jotted down his thoughts on sculpture, with particular emphasis on his great, unrealized work, the Sforza horse (see number 29). The discussions of sculpture also include detailed notes on heating and working with metal and alloys at various temperatures. Wouldn't it be great if every genius documented her thoughts so completely?

Every binder needs a few dividers

Leonardo's most formalized notebooks comprise *A Treatise on Painting*, but what about the other thousands of pages he wrote? They cover a wide range of subjects, including architecture, anatomy, zoology, physiology, astronomy, time, water, boating, musical instruments, fables, and stories. Leonardo may even have intended to turn his observations on various subjects, especially those sections on architecture, astronomy, and water, into entire books. Leonardo was, in many ways, a walking encyclopedia.

His notes range from almost boring, to completely out of this world. While some comments were pretty abstract, he also made useful suggestions. In one of his more practical moments, Leonardo notes any room or building that serves as a dance hall should be located on the ground floor, so as to avoid the danger of dancers stomping their way through the floor. Other portions of Leonardo's notebooks reveal his fascination with the process of conception—from a medical standpoint—and the layout of a fetus in the womb. He didn't stop there, though, and continued to chronicle the lives of people from infancy into the teenage years.

Leonardo's notes also contain pithy philosophical statements and maxims on such topics as religion, morality, science, mechanics, politics, speculation, spirits, and nature. His writings include a number of mathematical tricks and rebuses. In addition, he constructed a number of short fables, mostly featuring animals. He also wrote a variety of jokes and other amusing stories, such as this one:

> *"It was asked of a painter why, since he made such beautiful figures, which were but dead things, his children were so ugly; to which the painter replied that he made his pictures by day, and his children by night."* (*from* The Complete Notebooks of Leonardo Da Vinci, *translated by Jean Paul Richter*)

The majority of the text (without any pictures) of Leonardo's notebooks is available free online from Project Gutenberg. You can view or download the text from here: *www.gutenberg.org/dirs/etext04/8ldvc10.txt*

And the lucky winner is . . .

Upon his death, Leonardo probably wanted to leave his notebooks to a close personal ally, someone who would never sell them or lose them in the basement. And whom did Leonardo trust with this weighty responsibility? None other than his pupil and close friend Francesco Melzi. Leonardo's last will and testament reads, in part:

"The aforesaid Testator gives and bequeaths to Messer Francesco da Melzo, nobleman, of Milan, in remuneration for services and favours done to him in the past, each and all of the books the Testator is at present possessed of, and the instruments and portraits appertaining to his art and calling as a painter." (from www.gutenberg.org/dirs/etext04/7ldvc09.txt*)*

Since he had no wife, children, or other close relatives that we know about, Leonardo chose to leave the bulk of his estate to Melzi. Scholars believe that Leonardo left at least fifty (and perhaps as many as 120) complete notebooks to Melzi. Today, unfortunately, only twenty-eight survive in various versions. There aren't very many notes left from before 1500, so most of what's available are his writings from about 1500 up until his death in 1519. In addition to notes, there are also drafts of letters Leonardo composed as well as financial statements showing how much he was paid, or was owed, by various people.

After Leonardo's death in France, Melzi brought the pages back to Italy with him, keeping them with him until his death in 1570. There is some evidence that

Melzi attempted to organize and excerpt some of Leonardo's writings, as well, including discussions that became *A Treatise on Painting*.

By the time of Leonardo's death, unfortunately, much of his fame and reputation had been forgotten. He died as a recluse in France and didn't produce much in his final years. His choice of heirs didn't help much in spreading the word of Leonardo's good name—Melzi was a minor noble, but of little importance. When the notebooks were discovered after his death, their value was not recognized. Because of Leonardo's mirror writing, they appeared to be gibberish to the untrained eye, and many people probably thought they were mere scribbles. Melzi's heirs didn't help the situation much either—they left the precious documents in an attic! They later gave away or sold many of the individual sheets, without any idea of what they were actually worth.

It was through these various blunders and ignorance that Leonardo's notebooks, sketches, and writings became scattered. Many were probably discarded, and some of the remaining pages show notes in other handwriting in various places—meaning someone else (a monk, perhaps) made their own notes on top of Leonardo's. Can you imagine doing your homework on top of the *Mona Lisa*? Tragically, only a small percentage of Leonardo's prolific written output was saved, and these pieces have been collected over the years in volumes called codices. Probably the pages with particularly interesting sketches were kept more often than the pages and volumes with only text.

In the end, many factors doomed Leonardo's prolific scientific output to obscurity: his secretiveness in recording his observations, the lack of publication, and his many incomplete projects. Because very little of Leonardo's work was ever published or shared, his discoveries actually had little impact on the progress of science. How would anyone have known what Leonardo was think-ing if he never shared it with anyone? Scientific discovery and invention, in fields from military engineering to human anatomy, proceeded in the slow, steady pace typical of history—unfortunately, it proceeded without the benefit of Leonardo's great leaps of intellect. Maybe history just wasn't ready for Leon-ardo, but we'll never know because Leonardo gave so little of his work a chance to be studied!

Leonardo's notebooks were not studied in any systematic fashion until the nineteenth century, when some of the first translations were made. Historians tried to determine and restore the original order of the notes. It was also around this time that Leonardo's notebooks were first exhibited to the general public.

Because of his lack of influence on future generations of scientists, Leon-ardo is sometimes called the last of the ancient scientists (because of technologi-cal and political limitations, these scientists tended to work in isolation). Today, the progress of science is much more collaborative—scientific discoveries are all based on the theories that came before. A truly innovative thinker like Leon-ardo, who basically invented most of his work from the ground up, would have had a very different place in a modern scientific world!

Decoding the codices

About 5,000 pages of Leonardo's notes still exist today. Originally written on loose sheets of paper, these notes have been bound into notebooks called "codices." And what is a *codex*, you ask? It is, simply put, a collection of manuscripts. The word codex is a useful one to apply to Leonardo's books because they've been arranged into separate volumes; each codex has a name, and it's easy to identify which particular sheet belongs to which group. The modern arrangement of the codices is somewhat haphazard, though, and the current volumes probably bear no resemblance to the actual order in which Leonardo wrote them. He should have numbered his pages!

Perhaps the person most responsible for this erratic mess was Pompeo Leoni, a sculptor at the royal court of Spain in the seventeenth century. Leoni collected many of Leonardo's writings, but while trying to organize them, he cut and pasted pages from various notebooks and sections of Leonardo's writings, organizing them into separate volumes arranged into artistic, technical, and scientific sections. It messed up the original order, but at the same time provided us with a convenient cataloging system. From Leoni's efforts sprang the "Codex Atlanticus," and the so-called Windsor collection. Both of these codices are notable because they consist mainly of drawings and sketches that Leoni cut out of other places in Leonardo's writings. When Leoni died, some of the manuscripts were brought back to Italy, while others remained in Spain.

The "Codex Atlanticus" is currently located in the Biblioteca Ambrosiana in Milan. This volume contains hundreds of sheets of Leonardo's original notes, most of which date from between 1480 and 1518. The codex was donated to the library in 1637, but was taken to Paris along with other notebooks of Leonardo's when Napoleon conquered Milan in 1796. What a war prize! There, the notebooks were kept in the National Library of Paris and the Institute of France. In 1851 the "Codex Atlanticus" was returned to Italy, but twelve other manuscripts remained in France at that point. Primarily, the "Codex Atlanticus" contains the technical, mechanical, and scientific drawings from different notebooks, while the artistic, natural, and anatomical drawings are part of the collection at Windsor.

About 400 pages of the "Codex Atlanticus" are currently available online, although only in Italian at the moment! The site is *www.ambrosiana.it/ita/ca_principale.asp.*

Diving into the dusty library stacks isn't always a thrill, but the folks in Madrid are glad they did! Some of Leonardo's most valuable writings remained safe but unknown in the Biblioteca Nacional, in Madrid, until they were found by chance in 1966. These documents are now known as the "Madrid Codices." The two volumes include work on mechanics, dating from 1490 to 1496, and geometry, from 1503 to 1505.

Leonardo's other codices are located all over the world. Currently housed in the British Library is the "Codex Arundel," 238 sheets that were removed from various notebooks, forming a hodgepodge of drawings and notes. Leonardo started the collection in 1508, while he was living in Florence. While most of the contents come from around 1508, other pages were written at different points in Leonardo's life. The subjects include everything from mechanical designs to studies on the flight of birds. In this volume Leonardo also wrote that he had begun collecting various comments and sketches in one central location, which he wished to later reorganize according to subject. Of course, he never actually got around to finishing this project.

Parts of the "Codex Arundel" are currently available online from the British Library, in a shockwave format that allows you to turn pages and translate text, at this site: *www.bl.uk/collections/treasures/digitisation.html.*

A more minor codex, called the "Codex Trivulzianus," currently makes its home in the Biblioteca Trivulziana at the Sforza Castle in Milan. This selection of fifty-five sheets contains Leonardo's notes on architecture and various religious themes, as well as literary notes. These early works are thought to date from between 1487 and 1490. Another minor codex, called "On the Flight of Birds," is in the possession of the Biblioteca Reale in Turin. Consisting of seventeen pages, dating from about 1505, Leonardo used this codex to make a rigorous study of the details of flight, including wind and air resistance.

The only codex that is currently in the United States is the "Codex Leicester," written between 1504 and 1510. Software giant Bill Gates paid $30 million to purchase the "Codex Leicester" in 1995. Bet you didn't realize they even were for sale! This seventy-two-page codex consists of double-sided sheets of linen paper, and its main topics include studies of water, rocks, light, and air. Like most of Leonardo's works, it was done in Leonardo's signature mirror writing. The "Codex Leicester" was one of the few manuscripts not inherited originally by Melzi and, at the moment, is the only manuscript of Leonardo's that is privately owned.

Say cheese!

Portrait painting is in a whole other league from landscapes or religious scenes. Since you're trying to paint a real live person (most of the time), the painting actually has to look like that person! While caricatures are popular today, especially on boardwalks or street fairs, Renaissance royalty didn't want to see themselves with giant noses and ears. The artist had to have the skill to create a reasonable likeness. Then, of course, there was the difficulty of being the subject. He or she had to stay still for extremely long periods of time. Also, remember that portraiture is not the same as photography. The goal isn't just to create a mirror image of the original; the artist also has to capture some aspect of the subject's spirit, in addition to selecting a proper pose and background. Should the subject be nude or clothed, dressed to the nines or in everyday garb, sitting or standing, holding a favorite pet or other object, seated by a window or lying in a bed? The artists of the Renaissance had to go back and forth with the subject, making compromises but also ensuring the final painting was a good one. That's a pretty huge checklist—which is why portrait artists were few and far between.

Leonardo's *Mona Lisa* is a hallmark of portraiture because it captures the subject's essence so unforgettably. Leonardo's technical painting abilities helped him make her appear unfathomably real, but her eyes, mouth, and other facial features also give her a mystery rarely captured in a painting. But Lisa's portrait may not be as true to life as it seems. Modern-day historians have aligned the *Mona Lisa* with Leonardo's own self-portraits, showing that the features line up nearly precisely. Maybe this suggests that Leonardo included a bit of himself in his historic work!

In addition to the *Mona Lisa*, Leonardo created other portraits of women, including *Ginevra de'Benci* of 1480 and *La Belle Ferronniere* of 1495. He did paint male portraitures as well, but not nearly as many. One well-known male study was the *Portrait of a Musician* from 1483, which is also one of his best-preserved paintings. Ironically, we know very little about it—we don't even know who the person in the picture was! Some historians believe it to be Ludovico Sforza (see number 21) while others think it is Franchino Gaffario, Milan's most famous choirmaster.

Beauty cannot always be imitated, and the haunting beauty of the *Mona Lisa* was not to be repeated, though Leonardo's works are all originals. He made chalk studies of other wealthy individuals, some of which he probably planned to copy and paint later. Lack of interest (or perhaps the unavailability of the subject) seems to have prevented drawings such as these from reaching completion. While unfortunate, it's hardly surprising to see even more unfinished works from Leonardo.

In addition to portraits, Leonardo also sketched wanderers and gypsies. One of the most unusual of these portraitures is his *Grotesque Head* chalk drawing of 1504. He did a number of pen-and-ink caricatures in the 1490s, most of which show distorted facial features and hair. Biographer Vasari has addressed this dimension of Leonardo's work, noting that Leonardo was very interested in odd people and would often follow them, committing their features to memory. His original *Grotesque Head* image is nearly life-sized and seems to have set a trend; other painters around Europe soon began creating their own versions of grotesque portraits. It is possible that these drawings provided one of the earliest foundations for modern-day political cartoons.

It's like looking in a mirror

While Leonardo was busy with bigger (and better?) tasks, he did create several self-portraits over the course of his life that, in a prephotographic world, gave viewers some insight into his more personal side. Who isn't curious about what the great genius actually looked like? Fortunately, it's not such a mystery.

Not all of Leonardo's self-portraits are pretentious and formal. One of Leonardo's best-known self-portraits, dating to about 1512, contains his own annotations and was done in red chalk on paper. In this drawing, he has a full, flowing white beard and is clearly getting on in his years. Leonardo may have created several other sketches of himself, though it's a bit tricky to confirm that he actually drew them. One example is a sketch named *Old Man Sitting*. It's most likely from the late 1400s and appears to be Leonardo sitting along the bank of the River Loire.

Another example is *Profile of a Warrior in Helmet*, a silverpoint drawing Leonardo prepared in 1472. Given the time period in which Leonardo created this work, it is possible that this drawing was actually one of Verrocchio's models; it resembles similar figures in Verrocchio's bronzes and doesn't really look much like Leonardo. Some historians, though, believe that it was actually a self-portrait.

In addition to these standalone self-portraits, Leonardo also included himself in several of his most famous paintings. He was clever enough to sneak himself in as a bystander—the patrons probably never even knew Leonardo was in the paintings. One of the best examples is his *Adoration of the Magi*, into which most historians think he painted himself as one of the shepherds. The figure in question is in the bottom right corner of the painting, and the shepherd is facing away from the main crowd. Just another indication of Leonardo's slightly devilish sense of humor!

His self-portraits weren't just limited to paintings, either. In 1496 Leonardo illustrated a mathematics book for Fra Luca Pacioli (1445–1517), a mathematician who wrote several books on geometry, arithmetic, and proportions (see number 53). Leonardo may also have included a self-portrait of himself in the book *Divina Proportione* (see number 53).

While Leonardo enjoyed painting himself, he also extended this privilege to others, and at various points in his life, Leonardo posed as a portrait model. Verrocchio probably based his 1466 sculpture of *David* on a young Leonardo. Raphael likely used Leonardo as the model for Plato in his 1510 painting *The School of Athens*. Also around this time it is thought that Leonardo's student and companion Francesco Melzi drew a red-chalk image of Leonardo, as he would have appeared in his final years. Because the quality in this drawing is so high, it is thought that Melzi may have actually traced over a self-portrait Leonardo created a few years earlier.

Write to the point

When it comes to ancient arts, nothing goes back further than storytelling, and Leonardo dabbled in fiction writing, gracing us with a number of short stories. We're not even sure Leonardo wrote them all himself; some might be stories that friends of Leonardo wrote in his name, or stories Leonardo simply wrote down after hearing someone else tell them. Many of these stories are still told today, and most people don't even know they came from Leonardo da Vinci; they are simply known as Italian folk tales, beloved by children and adults alike.

Leonardo wrote at least thirty stories. Not bad for someone who wasn't even an author! As with his notes and sketches, he illustrated most of his stories. One of his first was a fable called "The Testament of the Eagle." As the story goes, an old eagle nearing his deathbed calls his children together and tells them that he is approaching the end of his life. He then describes how he intends to die: by flying so close to the sun that it will burn his feathers, thus sending him into the ocean. He will then rise from the water and begin life anew. Such is the life cycle of the eagle, at least in Leonardo's version!

Another of his famous fables was that of "The Spider and the Grapes." A clever spider, who sees how bees and flies feast on the sweet grapes of the vineyard, decides to spin its web right next to the grapes. Flies will get stuck in the web, and the spider will have a meal. One day, the vineyard owner cuts down this particular grape stem. The flies are rescued from their certain doom, while the spider is punished for his trickery. Like most of Leonardo's stories, there is a definite moral here: Preying on the innocent can lead to no good.

"The Mouse and the Cat" is another fable about intelligent animals. A mouse is trapped in its hole by a stalking weasel. While the mouse pleads with the weasel to leave, a cat, which has been lying in wait, pounces and devours the weasel. Thinking the coast is now clear, the mouse celebrates by rushing out of his hole—only to be promptly eaten by the same cat. The enemy of your enemy is not always your friend!

A final fable that was close to Leonardo's heart is "The Goldfinch." A mother goldfinch returns to her nest one day to find all her babies missing. She eventually discovers them caged and hanging outside a farmhouse window. Try as she might, she can't open the cage. The next day she returns to feed her babies through the bars. But they die soon after because their mother has fed them poisonous berries. Her final words: "Better death than loss of freedom." Perhaps Leonardo felt that if artists couldn't be free to design as they wished, then they shouldn't produce art at all?

Bringing down the house

Music was a very important part of the Renaissance, and as a child Leonardo showed interest in a diverse range of musical activities. Apparently, he was a good singer and liked to spend evenings entertaining friends and relatives. Singing was a well-respected pastime during the Renaissance; most educated people could either sing or play a musical instrument.

Besides singing, Leonardo taught himself to play the lyre, a stringed instrument that had been around since at least ancient Greece (though it was probably invented in Asia). A lyre looks a bit like a rounded harp and consists of a hollow body with two semicircular arms connected by a crossbar. Strings start at this crossbar, go over a bridge, and terminate at the opposite end of the lyre. They came in different sizes and with different numbers of strings, usually four, seven, or ten.

While Leonardo focused most of his attention on drawing, painting, and designing, he kept up his skills with the lyre, prompting Michelangelo, one of Leonardo's biggest rivals, to refer to Leonardo as "that lyre-player from Milan." During his patronage years with the Sforza family, Leonardo was sent to Milan to play the lyre for Ludovico Sforza. The soon-to-be duke had fought (and won) political battles to reach this new station in life, and a celebration was warranted. For the occasion, Leonardo brought a special lyre he had made himself. It was silver, designed in the shape of a horse's head—pretty spectacular, since most lyres of the day were of a simple wooden design. His performance was rumored to have been far better than those of the court musicians, endearing Leonardo to the royal family (but perhaps not to the musicians). He was also known for making up his own songs, complete with rhyming lyrics, on the spur of the moment. Perhaps he was the world's first improvisational artist!

Some historians think Leonardo not only played instruments, he helped design them, in particular an early predecessor to the violin. The Medieval period saw the development of stringed instruments with bridges. (A bridge is a vertical piece of wood that the strings are stretched across; they allow bowing in addition to plucking.) The first real predecessor to the violin is called the *viola de gamba*, which was first created in the fifteenth century and became more popular in the seventeenth century. During his lifetime, Leonardo built several string instruments, and his notes indicate an interest in studying their acoustical properties. Leonardo's studies in tone, sound, and related instrument properties surely influenced the artists who would go on to create the violin, cello, and other stringed instruments. Some of the first violins were created by Gasparo da Solo (1542–1609), and while da Solo was born after Leonardo's death, Leonardo may have had conversations with da Solo's father.

What fun is being a genius if there's no one to brag to? Leonardo's work was of legendary appeal, but he wasn't the only great Renaissance artist. Some of the others were his friends, some were his enemies, and some he barely knew. His most famous rivalry was probably with Michelangelo, creator of *David* and purveyor of the fig leaf. While these two legends competed for a variety of projects, fortunately, Leonardo's relationships with other contemporaries were more collaborative. For instance, he probably studied with Botticelli when both were apprenticed to Verrocchio's studio. Even though Leonardo had less interaction with other Renaissance artists like Titian, his own style and influence were pervasive.

Other Renaissance giants included Machiavelli, with whom Leonardo apparently had a cordial relationship. Machiavelli even recommended Leonardo for at least one commission! There's nothing like having friends in high places, and Leonardo always made sure to nurture relationships that would help his career.

In spite of Leonardo's wide range of interests, he was relatively ignorant of other major discoveries of the day, such as the heliocentric solar system of Copernicus and Columbus's discovery of the Americas. We don't have much record of these events in his notebooks and don't have any other way of telling how much Leonardo knew about world science and politics. However, it is likely that Leonardo was affected by the religious turmoil of the day, which gave rise to the Protestant

Reformation of Martin Luther and John Calvin. These events postdate Leonardo's career slightly, though the growing battle within the Catholic Church probably influenced him. Between indulgences and the Ninety-five Theses, it's hard to imagine that Leonardo could shove his head in the sand and ignore what was going on.

Although we can't know for sure what precisely Leonardo knew about the world around him, the response Leonardo invoked from his contemporaries is quite well known. Fortunately, history has been kind to his reputation and many different scholars have studied Leonardo, Freud in particular.

It should come as no surprise that Freud focused on Leonardo's psychosexual development, coming to some interesting (if not true) conclusions. What is it they say about opinions, that everybody has one? Freud expressed his loud and clear, and it makes for a very interesting interpretation of Leonardo's personal life.

Michelangelo:
The Renaissance's "other great artist"

Was anyone greater than Leonardo? A better painter, per chance? We're not saying, but Michelangelo Buonarroti (1475–1564) might! He was one of the major architectural/artistic forces in the Renaissance—in addition to Leonardo, of course. Michelangelo was born in Florence and apprenticed at age thirteen to painter Domenico Ghirlandaio. While working in the Medici's sculpture gardens, he began creating marble relief sculptures, which gave a glimpse into his future talent. He moved to Rome in 1496, where he sculpted such masterpieces as *Pieta* (1498–1500). His return to Florence was marked by his 1501 creation of the marble *David*, perhaps his best-known sculpture. Michelangelo then went back to Rome in 1505 at the request of Pope Julius II. After beginning design and sculpture on the pope's enormous tomb, he started work on the painting of the Sistine Chapel's ceiling. These intricately detailed scenes from the book of Genesis kept him busy between 1508 and 1512, as he spent days upon days painting on his back.

Around 1519 Michelangelo began to shift his focus to architecture. He designed a new façade for the Florentine Church of San Lorenzo as well as the abutting Laurentian Library. Between 1519 and 1534, he worked on the Medici Tombs, designing both the architecture and the sculpture within. He was in Rome again by 1536, working on *The Last Judgment* fresco for the Sistine

Chapel. Michelangelo's best-known architectural work was at St. Peter's Basilica. Like Leonardo, Michelangelo was related to the Energizer Bunny and kept going and going—despite his age! He was still an active artist late in his life, creating frescoes for the Vatican's Pauline Chapel.

There is nothing like good rivalry to make you want to work hard and succeed, and Renaissance artists were subject to more than a little healthy competition. There is even a rumor that Michelangelo may have mocked Leonardo about the failure of his massive equestrian statue of Francesco Sforza! While they knew each other by reputation, it appears Leonardo and Michelangelo may not have crossed paths until 1500, in Florence. The two had much in common; they were two of the most celebrated architects and artists of the day, and various ruling parties recognized their fame. Both created pieces of historic proportions, and both were prolific with their skills. Additionally, they were both leading the way in terms of anatomical research; their representations of animals and people were far superior to most of those done by their contemporaries.

Leonardo and Michelangelo had at least one project in common: At the Palazzo Vecchio, in 1503, both won commissions for murals to be themed with Florentine military victories. Leonardo's design was a representation of the Battle of Anghiari, a scene in which the Florentines defeat Pisa. Leonardo completed sketches for this painting, but unfortunately, the painting itself suffered from yet another of Leonardo's design innovations, and nothing remains of it today (see number 32). Michelangelo's mural would have represented the Battle of Cascina, but his also only remains in cartoon form since Pope Julius II called him away before he was able to create the actual painting. This project seemed cursed from the beginning! Michelangelo and Leonardo must have had at least one other run-in around this time, since Leonardo was on the 1502 committee to decide where to place Michelangelo's *David*.

The young master Raphael

Wouldn't it be nice to live in a world where you were the undisputed champion in all things, and there was no one to challenge your greatness? Unfortunately Leonardo didn't live in such a world. As one of the great artists of the Renaissance, Leonardo had some powerful rivals. One of the most famous painters during the fifteenth and sixteenth centuries was Raphael, or Raffaello Sanzio (1483–1520). Though he only lived for thirty-seven years and didn't produce the same volume of work as his rivals, Raphael created some of the best-known frescoes from the Renaissance period.

Like Leonardo, Raphael wasn't born with a silver spoon in his mouth. He spent his early years in the city of Urbino, where he was already becoming recognized for his artistic abilities. Around 1495, he moved to Perugia, and by 1502 he earned a commission to paint for the Oddi Chapel in the San Francesco church, from which he produced *The Coronation of the Virgin*. This painting was followed by *The Marriage of the Virgin* in 1504, which shows a detailed attention to both the perspective and the quality of the figures; they appear mobile, attentive, and genuinely involved in the scene.

By 1504, Raphael had moved to Florence. Could he have lived in ignorance of Leonardo's and Michelangelo's respective masterpieces? Probably not, and odds are that he moved there to work closer to these great masters. Leonardo's influence is evident in several of Raphael's paintings of the Madonna. These include the *Madonna del Prato* (1505), *Madonna of the Goldfinch* (1505), and *Madonna and Child with the Infant St. John* (1505–1507). Raphael typically used a rolling, somewhat fantastic landscape setting for his Madonna paintings, indicating that he had carefully studied Leonardo's emphasis on botany and nature. It appears that Leonardo's *The Virgin and Child with Saint Anne* served as a model for Raphael—many of his paintings imitate the figural style that Leonardo used in that work.

All good artists had to be willing to pack up and move on at a moment's notice, and Raphael was no exception. Pope Julius II called him to Rome in 1508, and off he went to create murals for the papal residency in the Vatican. His major paintings for this period include the *Stanza della Segnatura* and the *Stanza d'Eliodoro*. The size, quality, and attention to detail of these murals are truly remarkable. Their subject matters stems from both ancient Rome and the Bible. The walls are a living testament to the history, culture, and variety that characterizes the Renaissance.

Like Leonardo, Raphael was a true Renaissance spirit: He could do more than just paint and was determined to showcase his abilities. After Bramante's death in 1514, Pope Leo X gave Raphael more responsibilities as a court architect. The transition was natural, since Raphael was already working on St. Peter's Basilica alongside Bramante. He was then involved with excavations around Rome, searching for remains from classical antiquity. Raphael likely had much interaction with Leonardo da Vinci during this period, since he was also in Rome under the patronage of Giuliano de Medici (brother of Pope Leo X).

So how was Raphael different from every other great Renaissance painter? He set himself apart from the crowd with the overall tone of his paintings. While Raphael had a bright, upbeat and even lighthearted style, Leonardo (and Michelangelo) tended to portray the darker side of humanity.

Botticelli on a half-shell

The Renaissance art explosion made room for plenty of up-and-coming artists to crawl out of the woodwork. Along with Leonardo, another Florentine artistic force was Sandro Botticelli (1445–1510). His father was a craftsman, and Botticelli was surrounded by artistic culture his entire life. Like Leonardo, he went the apprenticeship route and had several masters early on, including Fra Filippo Lippi and Antonio del Pollaiuolo. Pollaiuolo was an engraver (an unusual choice of master for a young painter), and Botticelli got an unusual education there. Also like Leonardo, Botticelli worked in Andrea Verrocchio's studio for a time. Was it something in the water or was Verrocchio just an amazing teacher?

By the time he was twenty-five, Botticelli had his own workshop in Florence. While Leonardo worked for various rulers and popes over the course of his life, Botticelli stuck mainly within wealthy, powerful Florentine families such as the Medicis. He had a better reputation for finishing his projects and probably didn't have to keep switching employers! One of Botticelli's most famous portraits was of Giuliano de Medici. This painting, from 1475, is thought to be the most accurate painting in existence of this powerful Renaissance figure. It's more stylized than Leonardo's works, though, and it doesn't match the skill and technological mastery of Leonardo's works.

Like Leonardo, Botticelli also painted a version of the *Adoration of the Magi*. His version was commissioned for the Epiphany Chapel in the church of Santa Maria Novella. This tempera-on-wood painting is closer to completion than Leonardo's version and, like Leonardo's, contains a self-portrait of the artist amongst the crowd.

In 1482 Botticelli created his best-known painting, *The Birth of Venus*. It's studied in virtually every art history class today and is one of the most recognized icons of the Renaissance. This painting shows Venus standing on a shell as she rises from the sea and nymphs wait for her arrival onto land. Venus (also known as Aphrodite) was the ancient goddess of love; renowned for her beauty, she is rendered here with grace and elegance.

One of the things that makes Botticelli so interesting is that he painted both pagan and Catholic scenes with equal skill. On the Catholic side, he painted a beautiful series of Madonnas, including the *Madonna of the Pomegranate* from 1486. The colors are bright and the figures sharply defined; Mary is seen with a faint glow over her head. Botticelli also painted religious frescoes of saints, including *St. Augustine* (1480) and *St. Sebastian* (1473). In one of his few ventures outside of Florence, Botticelli went to Rome in 1483 to help decorate the Sistine Chapel. His presence was requested by none other than Pope Sixtus IV, and he went alongside Ghirlandaio, Rosselli, and Perugino as part of a team of artists. Their work along the walls took only a year; the Sistine Chapel is, however, much better known for its ceiling painted by Michelangelo.

Botticelli had a crisis of faith in his later years, and some historians think that he joined the religious reformation in following the teachings of Girolamo Savonarola. This priest (who was eventually excommunicated and hanged) was responsible for the 1497 Bonfire of the Vanities, in which he and his followers collected and burned items associated with moral weakness: mirrors, poetry, art, and anything that may have had a "pagan" association. While Botticelli's actual involvement with Savonarola would have been minimal, it is thought that he did begin to question Italy's heavily Christian influence.

A major difference between Botticelli and Leonardo can be seen in their travels (or lack thereof). Botticelli remained in Florence for much of his life and missed out on any sort of real multi-cultural experience. Leonardo, on the other hand, spent years in many different cities throughout his career. He gained exposure to critics, earning the respect and admiration of the clergy and powerful families. He observed people from many walks of life, learning the music and culture of his international contemporaries.

Titian: His own personal giant

Leonardo da Vinci spent most of his career working in Milan and Rome. However, he didn't have the market cornered on Italian art! Titian (1490–1576), another artistic hero of the Renaissance, was Venice's major player. Titian's work complemented Leonardo and the other Renaissance greats, though they may not have met during their lifetimes. These two giants, with a little help from their friends, created the aura of the Renaissance art that we know and admire today.

Titian (whose full name was Tiziano Vecellio) was born near Venice. Like most Renaissance greats, he was tagged to be an artist early in life and was apprenticed to Gentile Bellini. Later he was apprenticed to Gentile's brother, Giovanni. He worked on several different paintings with the Bellini brothers and based his own style around his masters'. Titian's first known work was a series of frescoes on the Fondaco dei Tedeschi. A variety of painters worked on these frescoes, so historians struggle to identify precisely which paintings were done by Titian. One that is usually attributed to him is the *Fête Champêtre* of 1510. The scene combines nature and mythology: Lush landscapes and herdsmen are seen next to nude Poetry Muses.

Titian's next works were frescoes for the Scuola del Santa, which represent scenes from the miracles of St. Anthony. These works also show a symbiosis between a highly stylized landscape and a humanlike God. Titian continued this theme in 1518, when he painted bacchanalia scenes for the palace of the Duke Alfonso d'Este. One of these, *Bacchus and Ariadne*, is especially representative of Titian's style; bright colors separate the figures in the scene, and he fully captures the wildness of Dionysus and his followers. Titian is perhaps best known for these paintings because he was one of the first to show the revelry of bacchanalia in a distinctly Renaissance humanist setting. His work demonstrates daring accompanied by amazing skill: a winning combination!

An interesting note is that Titian's use of color here (among many other paintings) is more dramatic and even more cutting edge than Leonardo's. Bright colors were expensive to create, so most artists used the pigments that were available locally. Working with Venetian raw materials, Titian developed both bright and dark colors that really grabbed (and still grab!) the viewer's attention. One of his shades of auburn is so original that it is known today as simply "titian."

In addition to paintings of frivolity set in the rural countryside, Titian painted a number of religious scenes. *The Assumption of the Virgin* (1516–1518) was one of his first works that was clearly non-Venetian in nature, which gave him more credibility with guildsmen and patrons from other areas. The apostles in the scene are rendered in powerful motion, similar to the religious painting style of masters such as Raphael. The force and tension in the scene became a distinguishing characteristic of Titian's later religious paintings.

As he moved further into his career, Titian's paintings reflected a calmer atmosphere. The *Venus of Urbino* (1538–1539) was done for a specific client: Guidobaldo della Rovere, heir to the Duke of Urbino. The *Venus* conveys an intimacy seen only rarely in other works. Titian was, like most other Renaissance painters, also a capable portrait artist. By 1516 he had been named the state painter of Venice, and in the 1540s he traveled to Rome to do a portrait of Pope Paul III (it is thought that he may have met Michelangelo during this period).

Toward the end of his life, Titian's style changed again. His later works such as *Rape of Europa* (1559–1562) and *The Flaying of Marsyas* (1575–1576) show an increasing formlessness; shapes blend together and his scenes, though representative, become more abstract. His work displays a progression that you don't see as strongly in Leonardo's more consistent work. Luckily for the history of Western art, we don't need to choose one or the other! These two artists together create a rounded picture of what was possible during the Renaissance.

81

Machiavelli: The literary prince of the Renaissance

Artists didn't carry the complete weight of the Renaissance on their shoulders. Poets, philosophers, historians, dramatists, and authors had their own parts to play. All these professions contributed to the increasing Renaissance interest in the humanities. Niccolo Machiavelli (1469–1527) was a poet-philosopher with a particular knack for pushing the boundaries of what was acceptable. Hmm . . . sound like anyone we know?

Educated in Greek and Latin, Machiavelli had deep roots in history and philosophy. He read the books in his father's library and was always interested in understanding how society's problems were based on historical events. Machiavelli was a Florentine at heart, devoted to enhancing and protecting the image of Florence as one of Italy's greatest cities.

Machiavelli's best-known work is *The Prince*, written in 1513 as a critique of Renaissance politics. According to his observations, the powerful Italian ruling families were essentially modified versions of Attila the Hun: They were instigators of invasions, attacks, and general corruption. Some historians believe that this treatise was based on the life of Cesare Borgia, one of Leonardo's many patrons (see number 22). In *The Prince*, Machiavelli tried to define rules for the politician: how to gain power and how to keep it. The work was, in many ways, a model of behavior for the selfish ruling families of the day.

Public response to *The Prince* was, to put it mildly, less than congratulatory. Many people thought Machiavelli was cruel and harsh in his judgments, most of which were probably true. He appeared to have been an ardent supporter of political families such as the Medicis, a view that was becoming increasingly unpopular. Machiavelli was ousted from Florence several years later, and though he wrote more treatises, he was not well-liked during his lifetime because of the negative public perception surrounding *The Prince*. Fortunately, history has taken a more objective view of his writings.

Leonardo, always one to seek out a fellow artist, was rumored to have been friends and business partners with Machiavelli. They probably met while working with Cesare Borgia sometime during the early 1500s. Both men were patriotic, and both considered Florence their home. Though their professions were different, their perspectives on Italian Renaissance humanism were remarkably compatible.

In 1503, the two friends collaborated on Leonardo's scheme to reroute the Arno River. This plan would have given Florence both a seaport and an entirely new role as a city. Machiavelli researched the project politically and militarily, coming to the conclusion that such a diversion would benefit all of Italy, and he actively promoted the plan to the governing bodies. Unfortunately this project never reached fulfillment, but Machiavelli's involvement surely lent credibility to Leonardo's scheme.

Leonardo and Machiavelli had another common project: the depiction of the Battle of Anghiari. Though Machiavelli helped Leonardo to obtain this commission, their recordings of the event differed. Leonardo's painting shows the success of Florence in claiming this medieval town from rival Italians. Machiavelli, rather than blindly praising the Florentines, writes of their confusion in battle and their less-than-skilled armies.

While Leonardo may have taken artistic liberties with this patriotic rendering, his freedom of expression complements Machiavelli's more factual recounting.

Talking about a religious revolution

The Church was, of course, the guiding light behind Renaissance painting and architecture, but even it was subject to considerable challenges. The strongest of these was the Protestant Reformation of the sixteenth century. While Leonardo played only a small roll in this revolution, it's impossible to discuss the Renaissance without at least mentioning this major upheaval.

The leader of the Protestant Reformation was a German named Martin Luther (1483–1546). He diligently studied various parts of the Hebrew Bible as a child and was skilled in several ancient languages. He attended the University of Erfurt, studying philosophy and law; his father wanted him to be a lawyer, so he appeased the old man by going to law school. However, Luther soon realized what he really wanted to be when he grew up. By 1505 he had joined the Erfurt Augustinian monastery, where he learned about a whole new side of religion. In 1507, he was ordained as a priest, and up until this time he seems to have fit into a monk's lifestyle quite well.

In 1509, he went to Wittenberg, where he taught philosophy and studied religion. His visits to Rome showed him first-hand how the Church was focusing more on money than religion. Church officials were selling forgiveness from sins such as theft, adultery, and even murder. These atrocities forced Luther to doubt the very tenets of his religion, and he found himself disregarding the rules of the monastery in search of explanations that he could justify and accept. He became increasingly critical of the Church, particularly with regard to the indulgences (forgiveness for sins) he had seen. In 1517 he made a list of these indulgences, dubbed the Ninety-five Theses, and reportedly tacked it to the door of the church.

He probably hoped to spark Church reform with this act, but instead it led to his excommunication in 1521. Seems harsh, but what else was a Renaissance church to do? Holy officials couldn't tolerate dissenters, so they did the next best thing: shoved them under the carpet. Luther is most famous for beginning the process of questioning the Church. He took a stand and, unfortunately, paid a heavy price for it. Luther was more than a religious critic, though. He also produced the first full translation of the Bible into German, publishing his version in 1522.

John Calvin (1509–1564), another major player in the Protestant Reformation, had a middle-class French upbringing and, like Luther, eventually became an Augustinian monk. He had been trained in law and humanism, in the full Renaissance spirit, and came out in strong favor of the views Luther set forth. In fact, his speeches are the main reason why Luther is famous today.

Around 1532, Calvin experienced a religious conversion of sorts and became more interested in religion than law. The French King François I saw him as a threat, and Calvin was forced to leave France in 1536. He officially severed ties with Roman Catholicism and moved to Geneva. Calvin did not want to abandon Catholicism or the Church; quite the contrary! The Reformers wanted to do just that: change the Church's sinful ways. While change is usually good, it isn't always appreciated, and Calvin's ideas simply weren't welcome.

By 1583, Switzerland had also had enough of Calvin's criticism; kicked out of the country, he was forced to move to Strasburg, where he worked for the reform movement and got married. In 1541 he returned to Geneva to set up a school for training reformed Christians (Protestants); this school eventually became the University of Geneva. It had an inauspicious start, perhaps, but it become a major university.

So what did this all have to do with Leonardo? While the main part of the Reformation took place after Leonardo's death, he was aware of the impending rebellion and its associated turmoil. He probably heard of the theses-tacking incident and was aware that his beloved Church was coming under fire. Did it make him more religious, more observant? Or did it feed his inner rebel?

83

Center of the universe

Still think that art was the only thing going on during the Renaissance? Prepare to be proven wrong. Science was a fast-growing field, and many discoveries were made that changed the course of the world, literally. Nicolas Copernicus (1473–1543) was one of the Renaissance's foremost scientists and astronomers. Born in Poland, Copernicus was trained in mathematics, science, and philosophy. In 1488, Copernicus learned the basics of philosophy and other humanistic fields in Wloclawek, attending the University of Krakow in 1491. His diverse education allowed him to study astronomy, mathematics, geography, and Latin. While Latin may not be the most exciting subject, he pursued in the study of languages and eventually read the treatises of ancient Greek and Roman mathematicians such as Euclid and Ptolemy.

Copernicus's crowning achievement was the development of a heliocentric model of the solar system. Earlier scientists had thought that the entire solar system revolved around the earth, a model known as the "geocentric view." Copernicus showed that the planets actually orbited about a point slightly offset from the sun. He also showed that the earth rotated about its own axis once a day, while revolving around the sun every year.

Not to accuse Copernicus of blasphemy, but this entire concept was heretical in the eyes of the Church, where God was the center and, therefore, so was Earth. For this reason, Copernicus did not publish his ideas until shortly before his death. Had he published them sooner, his death might have been hastened! A student named George Rheticus then took on the editing and publishing responsibilities.

Like Leonardo, Copernicus was a true Renaissance man. He studied many different fields and used them all in his research. He combined physics, math, and studies of the cosmos into a new field of astronomy; this area of research had been more or less dead since the early thirteenth century. Like most of his contemporaries, Leonardo had a geocentric view of the solar system, believing that the planets and celestial bodies rotated around the earth. Copernicus and Leonardo probably never crossed paths, and since Leonardo was championing the older view, he was probably not influenced much by Copernicus—or modern astronomy, for that matter!

Copernicus and Leonardo had at least one common bond: They both created a starting point. Leonardo developed techniques such as *chiaroscuro* and *sfumato*; he set the standard for his contemporaries, and most painters after him followed his example. Similarly, Copernicus laid the foundation for a correct understanding of the solar system. Johannes Kepler (1571–1630) and Issac Newton (1642–1727), major mathematicians and scientists in their own rights, took Copernicus's ideas and developed deeper, more accurate models of the solar system. Without Copernicus, we might never have made it to the moon; without Leonardo, your living room walls would be blank and cheerless. Three cheers for innovation!

Leonardo on the analyst's couch

"Leonardo da Vinci was like a man who awoke too early in the darkness, while the others were all still asleep." —Sigmund Freud

With all of his oddities and eccentricities, Leonardo is a psychoanalyst's dream. He has been studied by artists, architects, historians, inventors . . . everyone wants a piece of him. His expertise was virtually unmatched, and artists today study his work as if it were scripture. Is it any surprise, then, that psychoanalysts want to take a turn? Sigmund Freud conducted a thorough study of Leonardo's life, using his notebooks to figure out what could have made Leonardo the genius he was. Freud being—well, Freud—the analysis was certain to be of a sexual nature.

Freud became deeply involved in the life of Leonardo. He did a massive study of the Renaissance master in 1910 called *Leonardo da Vinci and a Memory of His Childhood.* As was his custom, Freud mainly studied Leonardo's sexuality. He came to the conclusion that Leonardo had homosexual tendencies because his mother wasn't around very often and, as a consequence, Leonardo lived with his father for most of his childhood. His father was frequently away on business, so Leonardo spent considerable time with uncles and other male relatives. His illegitimate birth, according to Freud, gave Leonardo an obsession with sex and sexuality. Perhaps true, but who needs an excuse for this particular interest? Freud's other big idea was that Leonardo idolized/desired his mother; becoming romantically involved with any woman would have, per Freud's analysis, been out of the question, thereby leaving homosexuality as Leonardo's sole recourse.

So how exactly did these facts contribute to Leonardo's homosexuality? While being gay was fairly common during the Renaissance, its practice was a crime that could be punishable by death. Freud's opinion was that Leonardo's many unfinished projects were evidence of sexual tension caused by his inability to fulfill his sexual desires in public. Boy, that's a good excuse for not finishing a project! Freud's study was the first comprehensive attempt to understand Leonardo's sexuality. Since sexuality certainly wasn't discussed openly during Leonardo's lifetime, we don't have any better information on the subject. If nothing else, Freud's work was the catalyst that allowed this very discussion to take place.

Part 6

THE WRITING ON THE WALL

Much of Leonardo's personal life is a historical black hole. Through his notebooks, though, we can assemble bits and pieces of his personality. Even more information can be gleaned from the writings of his contemporaries. History will find a way, and in this case, that way is found in his most personal journals—some of which were never intended to be made public.

In a world where there were few certainties, here are some facts. Leonardo was a vegetarian who loved animals. He was strikingly strong and handsome in his youth, enjoyed fashionable clothes, and had the voice of a songbird. He was fiercely protective of his private life, but he had good reason: In 1476 he was accused of having an affair with a young male model. He was actually thrown in jail and stayed there for two months before the charges were dropped! Appearing to have shown no sexual interest in women over the years, Leonardo was likely interested in men, particularly beautiful, young boys. Leonardo had long-term relationships with two of his students, Salai and Melzi, and both are generally assumed to have been his lovers.

While his artistic talent was obvious, he didn't have artistic heirs or followers—he was really one of a kind. Either that or he was just a terrible teacher! The world would have been dramatically different if he'd been able to pass on his scientific and engineering ideas. Most of his inventions were right on the money, not to mention way ahead of their time. Leonardo's secrecy and tendency to work alone, though, impeded his legacy. The disorganization of his notebooks and their dispersion after his death shafted his potential glory. Still, Leonardo is clearly the archetype of the Renaissance man, good at everything he put his mind to. To be fair, maybe Leonardo wasn't as good an engineer as he was a painter; given how skilled he was with a paintbrush, though, the art world came out a clear winner.

Vegetable soup for a gentle soul

Leonardo the Artist had a well-documented career. So did Leonardo the Painter, Leonardo the Architect, and Leonardo the Inventor. But what about Leonardo the Man? Leonardo was intensely private, and much of his personal life remains a mystery. Still, glimpses of Leonardo's personality have been revealed through his notebooks and from his contemporaries' observations.

Animals were an important part of Leonardo's life. He sketched and painted from nature frequently, studying animal movement closely to allow accurate representations. Later in life he performed animal dissections, learning ever more about anatomical systems and how they related to the whole body.

Leonardo was, by all accounts, extremely fond of horses. Horses were actually important to all Italians because they played essential military and civilian roles. Leonardo took great pride in the appearance and comfort of his animals; he realized that they were separate living creatures who deserved the same comfort and humane treatment as people. He even designed elaborate horse stables with archways and ventilation systems.

In keeping with this deep compassion for animals, Leonardo was a vegetarian, probably for most of his life. His notebooks and other writings even contain a few vegetarian recipes! He also mentioned vegetarian chefs by name, including Bartolomeo Platina (1421–1481), in his notebooks. Common vegetarian recipes of the day focused on innovative combinations of herbs and spices with vegetables and pasta.

He seems to have felt a particular kinship for caged animals. Perhaps he felt trapped by many of Renaissance Italy's conservative tendencies, or perhaps his motley upbringing led to his feeling stifled. In his adult life, he was known to purchase cages full of animals and set them free.

During the Renaissance, good looks were important. Handsome artists were more likely to secure patronages than those who weren't as easy on the eyes; equitable or not, the royal families of the day preferred to surround themselves with fine-looking craftsmen. Leonardo was in good stead in this regard, plus, he was comfortable around royalty and had no qualms about dressing to the nines; he clothed himself in fashionable gear and was known for his jokes, stories, lyre playing, and songs. While he was intensely private about personal matters, Leonardo was fully capable of working a crowd!

Generally speaking, Leonardo was regarded as a humanitarian. He was not known for fits of temper, and despite his inability to finish many products he was easy to work with and enjoyed collaboration. He was also kind to his servants; in his will, he remembered several of them. His will provided candles for a number of beggars to carry in his funeral procession; he was thoughtful enough to take care of these sorts of details. Leonardo was the sort of person who would have made an excellent friend: loyal, kind, and considerate.

86

Highly personal accusations

Some people write tell-all memoirs, while others keep their personal lives to themselves. Although we might wish that he had been a bit more open, Leonardo was always very secretive about his personal life. Though thousands of pages of his writings survive, he mentions almost nothing about his innermost thoughts and feelings. This intense privacy could date from an incident in 1476, at the very beginning of Leonardo's professional career as an artist.

In 1476, the twenty-four-year-old Leonardo was still officially part of Verrocchio's studio, but was beginning to take on outside commissions. On April 8, 1476, an anonymous accusation was placed in a wooden box, put up for this purpose in front of the Palazzo Vecchio, in Florence. Someone had accused Leonardo and three other young men of having a homosexual affair with a male model and suspected prostitute, seventeen-year-old Jacopo Saltarelli. A second anonymous accusation against Leonardo was made on June 7.

In Florence, homosexuality was common and not particularly stigmatized, and the authorities usually ignored such conduct. However, sodomy was a criminal offense, and once formal charges were made, they had to be prosecuted. Leonardo and the others were actually taken into custody by the authorities and held for two months in confinement.

Fortunately for Leonardo and the other three accused, the charges were dropped due to lack of conclusive evidence and witnesses. It is also possible that the powerful Medici family influenced the outcome; one of the other young men accused along with Leonardo da Vinci was Lionardo de Tornabuoni, a relative of Lorenzo de Medici. This acquittal was conditional, however: It only applied if Leonardo and the others were never again subject to a similar accusation.

Because of this scandal, Leonardo and the others ended up being targets of the "Officers of the Night" in Florence, a loosely run organization that was the Renaissance equivalent of a vice squad! This group, known as the Uffiziali de Notte in Italian, was created in 1432 specifically to find and prosecute crimes of sodomy. Florence was the first European city to have such an authority.

Perhaps due to the accusation, there is no record of Leonardo's work or even his whereabouts from 1476 to 1478, although it is assumed that he remained in Florence. Leonardo appears to have recovered his equilibrium by 1478, however, for it was in that year that he received his first official commission, *The Adoration of the Shepherds*. This work, while never finished, seems to have launched Leonardo on his way to becoming an acclaimed artist.

While Leonardo appears to have put the accusation of homosexuality behind him fairly quickly, it is also likely that it influenced him for the rest of his life. His general paranoia could have been expressed in his mirror writing, which served as a foil to casual observers. His grotesque drawings of gossiping village people show exactly what he thought of rumormongers. In his writings, he also mentions the spreading of malicious rumors as a highly evil trait.

Leonardo may have eventually left Florence, his home city, to escape the memory of such accusations. As a budding artist, Leonardo needed a solid reputation, and escaping the Florence rumor mill may have put him back on the right track.

Amigos, compadres . . . lovers?

Leonardo was not what you would call a playboy. He wasn't hanging out in bars, picking up gorgeous women. In fact, he didn't have any relationships with women that we know about. He did, however, have two long-term male companions during his lifetime. The first, Gian Giacomo Caprotti da Oreno, was brought into Leonardo's household in 1490 when he was ten years old. He had a changing role in Leonardo's life, though few details are known. Was he an adopted son, an art student, a servant, or an intimate companion? Given the indulgence that Leonardo showed him, and the length of their twenty-five-year relationship, it seems clear that he was much more than just a common servant.

Giacomo was quickly nicknamed Salai, which means "little satan," or "devil," and this fellow lived up (or down) to his nickname. Leonardo's notes describe his early antics, especially his thievery. Salai began stealing from Leonardo as soon as he moved in; he even stole the money Leonardo had given him to buy new clothes. Not exactly the way to repay someone's kindness!

Undoubtedly a large part of Salai's appeal, in addition to his apparently indomitable spirit, was his beautiful appearance. His long, blonde curls were a favorite with Leonardo, and a number of his sketches of Salai show off his fine features. In particular, Salai was likely the model for the young man in Leonardo's *Portrait of an Old Man and a Youth*.

Leonardo tried to teach Salai to paint, but he does not seem to have been particularly talented. Under Leonardo's tutelage, he did produce a few paintings, which Leonardo is rumored to have retouched. The affection between the two men seems to have been genuine, and Salai remained with Leonardo until almost the end of Leonardo's life, over twenty-five years. Many marriages today do not survive that long! In Leonardo's will, he left Salai a house and half of his vineyard.

Leonardo's second long-term companion was Francesco Melzi, a minor noble from Florence who joined Leonardo's household in 1505, at age fifteen. Melzi appears to have been a more talented painter than Salai, and less of a handful! Melzi was also supposedly a very handsome young man, like Salai.

A number of Melzi's paintings and drawings survive, including a portrait of Leonardo. Leonardo-inspired elements are clearly visible, but Melzi's work lacks depth. His paintings appear almost flat, and his sense of proportion is less well defined.

Melzi remained with Leonardo until Leonardo's death, upon which he became the executor of Leonardo's will. Leonardo left the bulk of his estate to Melzi, including his clothes, the paintings in his possession, and perhaps most importantly, his notebooks. Melzi faithfully kept the notebooks safe until the end of his life, around 1570, and is thought to have organized some of them into a longer version of *A Treatise on Painting*. Unfortunately, by the time of Melzi's death the importance of the notebooks had been forgotten, and they were scattered by Melzi's heirs (see number 71). Although no direct evidence exists to prove that Leonardo and Melzi had a sexual relationship, the fact that Leonardo named Melzi as his heir and left his precious notebooks in Melzi's care indicates the deep love and trust he felt for his former student.

Let's talk about sex

Today, celebrities' sex lives are fair game for tabloids, TV talk shows, and dinner table discussions. In the Renaissance, gossip was probably a similar occupation, although without the modern media frenzy the pace of the rumor mill was probably a bit slower. Many aspects of Leonardo's life indicate that he was most likely homosexual. It is likely that his two long-time companions, Salai and Melzi, were his lovers (see number 87). There are also indications of his sexual orientation throughout his work. Generally, Leonardo had to be careful with regard to his private life; Renaissance society was certainly not as liberal as modern-day San Francisco.

Leonardo never married, and he is never recorded as having shown any nonprofessional interest in women. He even expressed his disgust for male-female sexual intercourse in his notebooks. A famous quote from his notebooks reads:

> *"The art of procreation and the members employed therein are so repulsive, that if it were not for the beauty of the faces and the adornments of the actors and the pent-up impulse, nature would lose the human species."*

Leonardo drew both male and female nudes, but there are fewer female drawings and they are much less detailed. Unlike other Renaissance painters, who were prolific in their renderings of the female body, Leonardo produced only one formal painting of a female nude, *Leda and the Swan*. Leonardo's anatomical sketches also include drawings of both male and female genitalia. While the drawings of male sexual organs are detailed and accurate, the female genitals are depicted with less detail and accuracy; more often Leonardo used them for his medical studies. Perhaps Leonardo had more ready access to male models than to female ones, but this disparity could also indicate Leonardo's disinterest in the female body.

Some of Leonardo's drawings may also suggest, in a more symbolic manner, his distaste for heterosexual intercourse. Many of his sketches and paintings depict phallic rock formations and womblike tunnels and caverns, rendered to appear harsh and unappealing. Is this analysis the product of modern interpretation, or was it Leonardo's original intention?

In spite of Leonardo's seeming preference for the male figure, he did not always portray these figures as hypermasculine. For example, in Leonardo's famous work *The Last Supper*, St. John is very effeminate-looking and appears somewhat androgynous. This portrayal has actually led to talk that the figure at Christ's right is actually a woman, with some art historians speculating that the figure may have represented Mary Magdalene, not St. John. This scenario is particularly unlikely, however, given the Church's influence and the subsequently strict adherence to traditional renditions at that time.

While Leonardo clearly enjoyed painting and drawing beautiful men, it seems almost ironic that he also painted one of the most celebrated and beautiful women of all time with the *Mona Lisa*. Perhaps he was capturing the true inner beauty of the model, or perhaps the *Mona Lisa* is a subtle self-portrait of Leonardo himself as a woman!

Warning: Genius at work

So what makes a genius? We generally consider a genius to be someone who shows an intellectual prowess that makes him or her stand out from the crowd. Geniuses are extraordinarily skilled in at least one area; they're often outstanding in multiple fields. They also tend to have skills that come naturally—they create works of amazing impact with seemingly little effort.

Leonardo's genius is obvious. He was a skilled painter, architect, inventor, scientist, and geometrician. He designed animal stables and tried to reroute rivers. His interests and skills were diverse. But did he actually have *too* many artistic gifts? Many of his projects went unfinished, and many of his skills could have been further developed. If Leonardo had only been good at painting, for example, he probably would have finished more works and, in turn, these pieces might have been of an even higher quality. But because Leonardo was good at so many things, he simply did not have time to focus on all of them.

Rather than focusing on one particular art or skill, Leonardo chose to spend time with each of them—he was what is known as a polymath, someone who has myriad talents in many different areas. Essentially, he was good at just about everything he tried.

Unlike Leonardo, geniuses often choose a particular field in which to apply their talents. Albert Einstein (1879–1955) is often considered one of history's greatest geniuses, perhaps the greatest scientific mind of the twentieth century.

Einstein was known for his theories that revolutionized the study of space and time, developing the General and Special Theories of Relativity, which showed that space and time were not absolute as had once been thought. Hundreds of years earlier, Leonardo had also compared space and time in some of his writings; he noted that time could be divided into smaller and smaller pieces, just as a line could be infinitely divided into smaller and smaller lengths. He thought that a single instant of time could be considered as a point. Much later, it was Einstein who showed that space and time were not the invariant quantities that Leonardo, and most other scientists, had assumed them to be.

Like Leonardo, Einstein had varied interests, although they weren't quite as far ranging as Leonardo's. Also like Leonardo, Einstein enjoyed music, appreciating the mathematical order and harmony. Leonardo had his lyre; Einstein treasured his violin. Both geniuses based their science and theories on simple observations, ones that they could make with little equipment. Both asked questions and both sought answers. But even in light of history's most intelligent people, Leonardo's genius stands apart.

Minor errors of a major genius

"To err is human, to forgive divine." —Alexander Pope, *"An Essay on Criticism"*

This famous quote expresses something most of us know all too well: Humans make mistakes. Try as we might, we are never perfect. That's OK, though! Making mistakes is part of the learning process. Leonardo, being human, was no exception to this rule. Though it sounds trite, the old saying is true: Even geniuses make mistakes. Einstein, one of history's greatest intellectuals, was eventually proven wrong on certain parts of his theories. Leonardo also made several known errors. But did he let his mistakes rule his life? Read on to see how they affected his reputation.

Some of Leonardo's errors were due simply to lack of information. The precise nature of human anatomy, with all its functioning and interrelating systems, was only starting to be understood in the fifteenth century. Leonardo performed "autopsies" on cadavers and made careful studies, but he had no formal medical training and was likely missing the big picture. For example, Leonardo made several sketches of a woman's womb, complete with uterus, fetus, and umbilical cord. However, he misjudged the size and shape of the placenta, and actually drew it more like a cow's.

Along those same lines, Leonardo occasionally championed popular but flawed theories. He was, for example, a fan of physiognomy, which held that it was possible to determine a person's personality and character by studying his facial features and head shape. Barthelemy Cocles first published this theory in 1533, though the ideas had already been floating around for some time. This concept was, of course, fundamentally biased and had no basis in science. One of Leonardo's more technical mistakes concerns his design for a military armored tank. If you examine the details of his wheel system underneath the carriage, it is clear that the wheels would have actually been turning in opposite directions. The wheels would have spun harder and faster until the entire tank collapsed in a heap of metal and smoke. There are two theories about this peculiarity: Some think Leonardo genuinely made a mistake in the design, while others feel he probably made this error deliberately, to ensure that his design could not be stolen and copied later. You have to wonder, though, why he would go to all the trouble of sketching something, knowing full well it would never work?

One thing to remember about the errors in Leonardo's work is that, during the Renaissance, artwork was often done collaboratively. Others in his workshop may have actually done pieces that are attributed to Leonardo. He had a number of students throughout his lifetime, and their skills were less developed (and more prone to error). Consider, for example, the drawing of Isabella d'Este from 1500. The cartoon sketch for this portrait showed some of the figure, notably the arm, out of proportion; the musculature was also incorrect, and the figure would not have seemed lifelike. Given Leonardo's careful attention to anatomical detail, it seems likely one of his students made these mistakes in the sketch.

The vast majority of Leonardo's work was of superb quality and highly accurate. The only reason we're able to find these few flaws is because they stand out—his mistakes were few and far between!

Why be normal?

Lots of artists are known for their eccentricities. Whether they're wearing an off-fashion goatee or a lopsided beret, artists march to the beat of their own drums. The creative mind doesn't always follow convention, and society tends to give artists special dispensation to do things their way. Luckily, Renaissance patrons were somewhat tolerant as well. Leonardo exhibited several oddities in his mannerisms and artwork, none of which seriously detracted from his fame or popularity. In fact, his weirdness might have even added to his mystique.

As mentioned previously, Leonardo wrote in a kind of backward mirror writing, and there are several theories as to why Leonardo wrote this way. Some say that it was a code; he was very protective of his ideas, and he didn't want contemporary artists to steal his inventions or copy his sketches. In addition, some of his religious theories were not completely in keeping with the teachings of the Church, and he may have deliberately recorded his personal thoughts so that his patrons (and the clergy) could not easily decipher them. There were rumors that Leonardo, though apparently a practicing Christian, disagreed with some stories from Genesis; he probably would not have wanted to voice these dissentions and chose the mirror writing as a way to disguise his thoughts.

Again, being left-handed, writing backwards was simply easier and more natural. Many left-handed people find it easier to write from right to left, if for no other reason than to avoid the inevitable ink smudges.

During the Renaissance, some people believed that left-handed writers bore the mark of the devil. Though it's doubtful Leonardo himself believed that left-handers were evil, he probably felt some discrimination. The mirror writing, then, could have been Leonardo's own response to the idea that being left-handed was somehow worse than being right-handed. One thing is fairly certain: Leonardo probably did not write this way because of any severe mental impairment, and he appears to have known what he was doing. When he had to write notes for his patrons or others in the general public, for example, he wrote in the traditional left-to-right style. Leonardo the switch hitter!

Leonardo's eccentricities extended beyond his handwriting style. He often took liberties in his paintings that more traditional artists might have avoided. Leonardo was, in his own way, a risk taker. While he had to keep up a certain amount of convention to please his patrons, he bent the rules whenever possible. For instance, in his painting *Annunciation* (1487–1485), the angel's wings resemble an actual bird's wings. Leonardo may have wanted to experiment with his animal drawings, but the result is that the wings seem oddly out of synch in this otherwise religious scene. It seems clear that Leonardo's own study was of more importance than the work's final appearance, and this unconventional attitude would definitely have made *Annunciation* something of an oddity considering the Renaissance emphasis on both beauty and harmony. Eccentricities of this sort might not have been tolerated with lesser artists, but in Leonardo's case they only served to increase his appeal.

Crazy like a fox

Leonardo was different. Very different! His ways of thinking and working were dissimilar from other people, both during the Renaissance and today. Since doctors love to study people who are different, a variety of twentieth-century mental health professionals have tried to diagnose Leonardo with various illnesses. The diagnoses range from more common ailments, such as dyslexia and attention deficit hyperactivity disorder, to more exotic conditions, such as bipolar disorder (formerly known as manic-depressive disorder). Was Leonardo certifiably nuts?

Attention deficit hyperactivity disorder (or ADHD) is a relatively new diagnosis, but the fact that it has only recently been defined does not mean people throughout history haven't suffered from it. Classic signs of ADHD include being easily distracted, often failing to finish projects, and frequently shifting from one activity to another. However, you will also find these characteristics in many creative people, who often have a large range of interests and switch frequently from one to another.

Leonardo certainly fits the pattern of finishing little that he started. He left behind many incomplete paintings and other projects he never even started! Leonardo explained his apparent inability to finish things by stating his range of interests was so large and varied he simply had too much that he wished to do. Perhaps Leonardo's flitting from one project to another indicates symptoms of a disorder like ADHD, but was really just one more element of his brilliant, albeit unorthodox, mind.

Some people think writing from right to left was Leonardo's version of a code, to keep his notes from prying eyes, but it could also be a sign of a different trait: dyslexia. Dyslexia is a learning disorder that causes you to transpose the locations of letters within a word, or write individual letters backwards. It can also cause difficulties in reading; dyslexics can see words as a jumble of letters in a mixed-up order, rather than a particular pattern.

Many dyslexic people who are left-handed actually write in a backwards mirror writing similar to Leonardo's. Some dyslexic people who write like this do it entirely unconsciously. Leonardo's spelling was often strange and erratic. Another trait of dyslexia, it could also be another result of Leonardo's self-education.

People in general seem to favor one of two thinking modes: Either they are verbal or visual thinkers. Some preliminary research seems to suggest that those who are dyslexic often have enhanced visual-spatial thinking skills, which would go along with a particularly visual method of seeing the world, rather than a verbal one. Leonardo would seem to fit this pattern. His notebooks pioneered the method of technical drawing in which the pictures were actually the main point of the work; this technique stood in contrast to more traditional works, where sketches served only to illustrate the main text. Leonardo was certainly a particularly gifted visual thinker. Perhaps the seemingly disorganized verbal output of his notebooks, and his unorthodox method of writing, were just consequences of the way his brain worked.

A third modern diagnosis that has been applied to Leonardo is bipolar disorder. This psychological condition produces periods of manic behavior, during which the individual is full of ideas and enthusiasm and often works nonstop on various projects. These periods alternate with times of depression, where the individual seems unable to accomplish anything.

It is possible that this condition could explain some of Leonardo's behavior. Reports of his work habits indicate that he did go through long periods of not working, followed by times of obsessive work where he would toil on a project day and night. Observers particularly reported this behavior during Leonardo's creation of *The Last Supper*, when he would stay away from the site for days at a time, then arrive and work furiously on a tiny portion of the painting. Other times he would arrive, stare at the work for hours, then add a single brush stroke and leave again. This sort of behavior could certainly be a hallmark of a bipolar-type disorder, but then again it could also just be a typical artistic temperament!

Despite any modern psychological diagnosis that you might try to apply to Leonardo, it is clear that he was a supremely talented and productive individual. Perhaps we should think of him as an example of what can be done if you focus on your gifts, and not your shortcomings!

More than meets the eye

Wit plus intellect: What better combination to create an artistic web of mystery? Add that to Leonardo's passion for humor and secrecy, and you've got the makings of code-riddled art full of hidden meanings. And what are the answers to Leonardo's puzzles, you ask? The riddles buried in his works range from object placement, to more outlandish claims of secret coded messages. The question is, how many of these codes are really there, and how many are the fictionalized inventions of overzealous art critics? You be the judge!

Leonardo seems to have loved puns, and many of his paintings include backgrounds or other elements that are puns on the name of the person being painted. One of his earliest known paintings, *Ginevra de'Benci*, is a portrait of a young woman, probably painted to celebrate her marriage. The woman is posed in front of a large juniper plant, which was a symbol of chastity. Yet Leonardo has sneakily included another reference here: The word for juniper in Italian is *ginevra*, so the plant in the painting is also a pun on the young lady's name.

Another of Leonardo's early paintings, *Lady with the Ermine*, contains a similar pun. The woman in the painting is thought to be Cecilia Gallerani, a mistress of Leonardo's patron at the time, Duke Sforza of Milan. The ermine that the young lady holds was a symbol of Sforza's court and appeared on his coat of arms. Thus it was a logical choice to appear in the painting. However, the addition of an ermine also has more subtle underpinnings that reveal Leonardo's sense of humor. An ermine, with its pure white coat, was considered a symbol of chastity, making the ermine an ironic choice to place with the duke's mistress. In addition, the Greek name for ermine is *galee*, which makes the animal's inclusion another clever pun on the young lady's name.

In another instance, Leonardo designed a huge forest scene on the walls and ceiling of a room in Sforza's castle. It's thought his students painted this room, dubbed the *Salla delle Asse* (Tower Room), based on Leonardo's design. In addition to the various symbols of Sforza's family, including intertwining branches to symbolize his marriage, the inclusion of numerous willow trees is actually an allusion to Leonardo's hometown of Vinci, which has "willow" as one of its meanings.

As you can probably tell, symbolism was prevalent among Leonardo's works. Some objects, such as a carnation or a lamb, may seem random until you know the underlying religious significance. For instance, take Leonardo's early work *Madonna of the Carnation*, which shows Mary holding a carnation out for the infant Jesus: Since the carnation was actually a symbol of the Passion, its inclusion makes perfect sense. Another similar Madonna and child painting, *Madonna with the Cat*, shows the mother and child holding a cat. The inclusion of the cat comes from a story that a cat gave birth at the same moment Mary gave birth to Jesus.

Leonardo's most famous work, the *Mona Lisa*, is full of symbolism. The veil that the woman wears could symbolize widowhood. It could also symbolize chastity, which would have been appropriate for a married woman. The winding path shown in the background behind her could be the so-called path of virtue (from a myth about Hercules), and if so would indicate that Lisa was most likely a wife, not a mistress. It has also been suggested that the Mona Lisa is actually a self-portrait of Leonardo as a woman!

Leonardo's interest in codes and hidden messages has caused people to scrutinize his works, especially the *Mona Lisa*, for any sign of hidden meaning. For instance, Lisa's dress has a neckline with numerous small detailed loops, and these loops have been searched for any signs of hidden meaning, to no avail. Historians have also searched the sheet music held in *Portrait of a Musician* for hidden puzzles, but without success.

"R-e-s-p-e-c-t"

Socrates once said, "The way to gain a good reputation is to endeavor to be what you desire to appear." Clearly, Leonardo endeavored to be quite a lot during his lifetime, from artist to architect, and everything else in between. So how did he appear to his contemporaries, and were their feelings about him different from our view of him today?

Leonardo was a Renaissance celebrity. At the time, his popularity must have been like a modern-day rock star, actor, and best-selling novelist all rolled into one. How did Leonardo build up this reputation, and what kind of influence did he have on the generations to come? Was his genius enduring, like the Beatles, or fleeting, like the Monkees?

Leonardo was especially esteemed as a painter; even with his track record of seldom finishing paintings, he was sought after for commissions throughout his life. He was also held in a position of high esteem as an engineer, especially during his years with Duke Sforza and Cesare Borgia. In contrast, Leonardo's scientific pursuits seem to have been more solitary. Because his anatomical drawings required the dissection of cadavers, a practice forbidden during his time in Rome under the patronage of the pope, this work had something of an illicit nature that, combined with Leonardo's general secretiveness, likely made him even less inclined to share it with others.

Today, Leonardo is largely remembered and celebrated as a painter—his masterpiece *Mona Lisa* is one of the most recognized paintings in the world, gracing everything from postcards to mousepads. His other works aren't known as well, perhaps because many of them were unfinished or poorly preserved. Still, the handfuls of surviving paintings that remain today are sufficient to cement Leonardo's place as one of the most masterful artists of all time. The limited quantity of paintings, along with their mysterious, haunting nature, seems to increase both Leonardo's mystique and the desirability of his preserved works.

In large part because of Leonardo's secretive nature, few of his inventions or scientific discoveries have had much historical influence. Most of his inventions were never built; rather than sharing his plans and designs with others, Leonardo kept them to himself. There is evidence he planned to publish his notebooks at a later date, but this was yet another project that Leonardo never finished. Coupled with his notebooks' codelike mirror writing, which likely caused their value to go unrecognized after his heir Francesco Melzi's death, Leonardo's caution in sharing his discoveries led to the dispersion and loss of much of his work.

Leonardo could have rightfully taken his place as one of the fifteenth century's primary innovators, ushering in a new age of invention and innovation in the Renaissance. Instead, Leonardo stands in history as a man both ahead of his time and out of step with the world around him. It is astonishing to look at the creations in his notebooks, some of which were not reinvented for 500 years!

His notebooks contain many inventions that the techniques of the time were simply too crude to build, and others whose importance was just not recognized. His design for a bicycle, assuming that it wasn't merely a modern hoax, is eerily similar to modern bicycles, right down to details such as the chain assembly. Leonardo's invention of a multibarreled gun wasn't reinvented until modern times. His helicopter design was also remarkably innovative for the sixteenth century. In fact, a skydiver tested Leonardo's parachute in the year 2000 and found it worked perfectly. Unfortunately, in Leonardo's day, it just wasn't possible to get up high enough in the air to test it properly!

Due to his idiosyncrasies, as well as the progression of society at the time he was born, Leonardo truly stands as a man out of time. It's too bad that much of his work was not publicly available, since some of his inventions surely would have changed the course of history. It seems the Renaissance world just wasn't ready for many of his innovations.

Sincerest form of flattery

If Leonardo was truly such a genius, who wouldn't want to study with him? Lots of students seem to have tried, hoping that some of the great master's genius would rub off on them. Unfortunately, while Leonardo was certainly good at doing what he did, it's not clear that he was so good at actually explaining what he was doing. One of the downsides of genius is that it's hard to share.

At various points in his life, Leonardo had a studio or workshop full of students, assistants, and apprentices. Especially during his long stay in Milan, Leonardo appears to have had quite a number of students associated with his work. Most artists at the time had workshops full of students, and you can see the influence of the teacher in many of their works. Yet Leonardo's style proved more than just a new method to copy, and none of his students seems to have fully mastered his complete technique.

Many copies of Leonardo's works exist. This artistic plagiarism is actually fortunate because in some cases, as with *Leda and the Swan* and *Madonna of the Yarnwinder*, Leonardo's original has been lost over time. Other works by students in Leonardo's studio bear trademarks of Leonardo himself, and it is easy to imagine the master reviewing the unfinished paintings of his students. He may have even applied his own brush to a troublesome area in order to demonstrate a technique to his students.

One such painting, which is clearly not by Leonardo yet bears some traces of his style, is *Portrait of a Young Woman*. This painting, a stiff profile view, is utterly unlike the naturally posed three-quarters views Leonardo favored in his portraits. It was most likely painted by Leonardo's collaborator and student Ambrogio de Predis between 1495 and 1500. Yet some details of Leonardo's influence are visible in the young woman's elaborate headdress, as well as her pearls and elegantly tied ribbons. Leonardo was particularly known for his skill in painting knots.

Leonardo's influence clearly helped de Predis; during his time in association with Leonardo he produced his two best works, the portrait mentioned above and a portrait called *Bartolommeo Archinto*. Unfortunately, after he left Leonardo's studio de Predis's talents seem to have sharply declined, and he produced little of interest for the rest of his career.

A similar story applies to many of Leonardo's other students. One of his more successful, Francesco Melzi, seems to have had a talent for copying Leonardo's paintings, but produced little of note on his own. Other students and imitators, such as Bernardini Luini, managed to portray the outer trappings of Leonardo's work in their own compositions, but their paintings seem flat and lifeless when compared with the subtle complexity of Leonardo's works.

Perhaps Leonardo's genius was too great, or his talent too far-reaching, for him to truly inspire and train artistic heirs. Many have tried to imitate Leonardo, with little to no success. The simple elements visible in his works—the enigmatic smile and the misty, fantastical backgrounds—are easy to replicate; however, the sense of depth and inner serenity of a work like the *Mona Lisa* is much more difficult to capture. Leonardo's paintings have an inner wisdom, as well as a darkness to them, which makes them more than just colors on a canvas. When you view them, they seem to come alive.

No records of Leonardo's methods or techniques as a teacher exist. It is possible to imagine that with his immense talents and natural abilities, he might have had difficulty explaining the basics. Concepts that were obvious to Leonardo were probably less intuitive to a group of talented (but not genius) apprentices. Though Leonardo tried, it doesn't appear that he was able to fully convey the nature of his work to his students. As a result, though Leonardo worked with many aspiring artists, he had no real artistic heirs. No one before or since has been able to produce the signature genius and mystery of a Leonardo original!

A horse of a different color

Imagine a twenty-six-foot-tall bronze horse and rider. If it would be spectacular today, imagine how amazing such a sculpture would have seemed 500 years ago! One of Leonardo's greatest disappointments could have been that his massive *Statue of Francesco Sforza* (see number 29) was never built. Leonardo's larger-than-life masterpiece from 1483 would have been the biggest equestrian statue on the continent.

Leonardo made many study sketches for this project and also made a large-scale clay model. Unfortunately, Leonardo's bronze was swiped by the military, who needed it to make silly things like cannons. French soldiers ultimately destroyed the clay model in the early sixteenth century when they used it for target practice.

Now, fast-forward 500 years to an American airplane pilot named Charles Dent reading about the destruction of Leonardo's clay masterpiece in a 1977 *National Geographic* article. Creating this horse sculpture quickly became Dent's obsession; he felt it would honor both Leonardo da Vinci and all of Milan. He wanted to donate the sculpture to the people of Italy in celebration of Leonardo's achievements. Dent, an amateur sculptor, set to work creating his own scale model of the horse.

In order to fund his project, Dent created Leonardo da Vinci's Horse, Inc., a nonprofit group dedicated to raising funds to cast the enormous equestrian work. When he died in 1994, Dent bequeathed a large amount of money to this foundation. From that point on, the project took off at a rapid pace. The group gathered funds in later years by selling smaller-scaled reproductions of Leonardo's horse.

Eventually, a smaller model of the horse was sent to the Tallix Art Foundry for casting. Numerous problems surfaced, though, so the Foundry decided to start over. The master sculptor was a woman named Nina Akamu. She had been trained in Renaissance art and sculpture, and was keenly interested in seeing the project completed. She spent at least a year researching the project, then another year creating a new scale model. This model was then upsized at the Foundry to create the final bronze sculpture. Akamu and her team proceeded to build a fifteen-ton, twenty-six-foot bronze of Leonardo's design. The similarity to the original work was retained, and observers later commented that the strength, poise, and force of Leonardo's original red-chalk drawings were preserved in the Foundry's replica.

In deference to Dent's wishes, the magnificent sculpture was sent to Milan. The giant horse had to be split into seven pieces for safe travel and welded back together in Italy. It was unveiled there in September 1999, where a grand ceremony accompanied its unveiling to the public. Since Akamu's horse was actually cast twice, a second copy resides at the Frederik Meijer Botanical Gardens and Sculpture Park in Grand Rapids, Michigan. This version is known as the "American Horse."

The Frederik Meijer Botanical Gardens and Sculpture Park is owned by the same Frederik Meijer who created the national grocery chain stores. Check out *www.meijergardens.org* for details.

In the beginning, there was religion

Many of Leonardo's paintings concern religious subjects, but what did Leonardo actually think of religion? Was he a true believer, or was he just another sheep in the flock?

Most scholars think that Leonardo was a practicing Christian. He spent much of his life working under the pope's influence, so his frequent meetings with the clergy probably influenced him. The facts here, though, are few and far between. Little is known about Leonardo's religious upbringing. His grandfather arranged for his baptism, and the church of Santa Croce is said to contain the font where Leonardo was baptized. That fact alone supports the possibility that he was indeed raised in the Christian tradition. There is nothing to suggest that Leonardo's father was particularly religious. Some of Leonardo's early training may have come from local priests, but that is also not known for certain.

Given that Leonardo's grandfather appears to have been a religious man, it is likely that his father was at least nominally Catholic, and his mother was either Catholic or Jewish. What we do know is that Leonardo wasn't averse to painting biblical subjects. *Baptism of Christ*, *Annunciation*, and *Madonna and Child with a Pomegranate* are just a few examples of the religious themes Leonardo was commissioned to paint. Given the time and place, though, he probably didn't have any choice. Religion, power, and culture overlapped significantly during the Renaissance, and support of the clergy was an important part of any patron's lifestyle.

At least one aspect of Leonardo's religious beliefs is certain: He believed in a God. His writings refer to God as the creator of the universe, and the heartfelt spirit of his religious paintings reveals his devotion. Although Renaissance humanism promoted the spirit, determination, and abilities of man, it also tied man's development to ongoing worship and religion; Leonardo embraced all these aspects of the Renaissance.

While not an out-and-out heretic, Leonardo did act in ways that you could call "free-thinking." The fact that he may have included images of himself in several of his paintings (including *Adoration* and *The Last Supper*) could have annoyed the religious orders, since scenes representing holiness did not usually include mere mortals.

His vegetarianism also made him stand out from the crowd. In Leonardo's day it was thought that God gave man free reign over the animals, and choosing to abstain from their consumption might have been seen as offensive to God. Vegetables in general were looked upon with suspicion, particularly root vegetables, which grew under the ground (in the devil's habitat). His eating habits notwithstanding, Leonardo did respect some traditional religious boundaries. He does not appear to have delved into magic, astrology, or other "black arts" of the day.

Leonardo's will also made provisions for a Mass to be said in his honor. Candles were to be lit in a number of different churches. In addition, upon his deathbed Leonardo repented for his sins and asked to be instructed in the last rites of Catholicism. He seems to have felt that he had much to repent for, but ultimately he professed his commitment to God.

It's all in the name!

Leonardo da Vinci is, for all practical purposes, a household name. In some form or another, his works have found their way into almost everybody's education. While Leonardo had a large number of lesser-known works, such as his inventions and sketches, his most famous works are extremely well known. In fact, *The Last Supper* and the *Mona Lisa* are two of the best-known paintings in history! Just check out the crowds of people in the Louvre, surrounding a small painting encased in a huge bulletproof, climate-controlled glass enclosure!

While Leonardo is most famous for his paintings and other designs, he has taken on a secondary fame through modern-day adaptations of his name. Perhaps the most current reengineering of the Da Vinci name is in Dan Brown's 2003 novel *The Da Vinci Code*. The focus of this mystery novel is on solving a murder; clues are revealed through Leonardo's works, which, Brown asserts, are full of hidden meanings and cryptic messages. In addition, Brown explores an ongoing rumor that Leonardo may have belonged to a secret society that was devoted to hiding the "truth" about Christianity. While this book is entirely fictional, it certainly has spurred interest in the Renaissance master!

Another recent usage of Leonardo's reputation can be seen in the motion picture *Mona Lisa Smile*. This feature film from 2003 is about a professor in the

1950s who used some unconventional teaching methods in order to encourage her students to think on their own.

Why did this movie choose to use the *Mona Lisa* as an analogy? One of the most powerful aspects of Leonardo's painting is the woman's smile; it is mysterious, inviting, and subtle all at the same time. Similarly, the main characters in the movie, students at Wellesley College, seem perfectly behaved by all outward appearances, but it turns out, not all of them are who they appear to be on the outside.

Leonardo's name also has made it onto Broadway! Well, off–Broadway. In 2003, Mary Zimmerman of the Berkeley Repertory Theater put on a production called *The Notebooks of Leonardo da Vinci*, in which she used writings from Leonardo's notebooks to piece together the fragments of Leonardo's known biography into a production that captures his dramatic strengths and greatest triumphs.

In sickness and in health

Today, if you're sick, you take some Tylenol or go to the doctor, expecting to get better and back to work in a day or two. In the Renaissance, though, sickness was more of a life and death matter. Illnesses that we can quickly get rid of today by popping a few antibiotics were a serious affair, and people often died from relatively minor bugs or injuries.

Fortunately for us, Leonardo appears to have led a generally healthy life. He didn't succumb early to illness, as did so many people in the fifteenth century. His vegetarianism may have contributed to this good health, since he does not seem to have had any trouble with his heart or other major organs. Of course, most people didn't live long enough to worry about things like heart attacks.

Leonardo was also rumored to have been very strong. He had well-defined musculature and was known for his physical appeal. Supposedly, one of his favorite "party tricks" was to bend a horseshoe using only one hand. He was proud of his strength and it probably came in handy; working with heavy wooden panels could not have been easy, and any young painter would have had to make and carry his own supplies. In addition, traveling with Cesare Borgia's army required large amounts of physical labor, and he had to be in good shape just to keep up with the warriors.

Life expectancy in the Renaissance was around forty years. By living to sixty-seven, Leonardo far exceeded the average for his time. Who knew that creating art was good for your health? Actually, his profession probably did have something to do with it; he wasn't out plowing the fields, fighting in battles, or otherwise doing things that might have shortened his life. However, at least one major illness did strike him. In 1513, Leonardo was working for Giuliano de Medici in Rome. Between 1513 and 1516, Leonardo was quite sick and did not produce much new work.

In addition to battling medical problems, his work does not appear to have been going well during this period. Leonardo worked on creating new types of paint and developed a few ideas for puzzles, but did not produce many pieces of art. His notebooks reveal this frustration, as he comments that he very much wanted to keep producing art despite his failing health. A letter to Giuliano de Medici from 1513 indicates that both Leonardo and his patron were suffering from illness at this time, and that while Leonardo was pleased that de Medici's health was improving, he wished he could have hastened his own recovery.

In 1516 Leonardo moved to France where he worked under his final patron, King François. He is believed to have had a stroke around 1516; some historians think that it caused a partial paralysis of Leonardo's right hand. Though he was not required to do any commissioned work during his final years, Leonardo still had full use of his left hand and spent considerable time sketching and working on his notebooks. Even a potentially devastating illness could not completely slow down Leonardo, nor could it cease his artistic activities.

Leonardo's health became progressively worse in his last few weeks. Some reports suggest that King François sat by Leonardo during his death, holding his hand and offering final words; other reports, however, indicate that the king wasn't at his royal palace on the day of Leonardo's death. During his final days, Leonardo amended his will, taking care of his final religious and civic responsibilities.

Leonardo da Vinci: The Renaissance man

You can't have a Renaissance man without the Renaissance! Obviously the term was unknown before the Renaissance, and it slowly started to be used in the following centuries. Today it's a pretty well-known expression, and Leonardo da Vinci's name inevitably comes up when you start talking about Renaissance men. So, you might ask, what exactly are they? Was there an application to fill out? Did it require special licensing?

Although there were no such requirements, the title was not liberally applied. Before the Renaissance, the Medieval period (which lasted from about 1200 to 1450) had its own distinct culture. At that time, the arts were much more generalized than they are today. There were no sharp divisions between fine art, architecture, and other crafts. The apprentice-based educational system meant that young artists learned a wide range of skills, rather than being pigeonholed early on. A strong architect was also expected to be talented in visual arts, tapestries, woodworking, sculpture, and all the other crafts required to create projects.

In the fifteenth and sixteenth centuries, as the Renaissance took hold, the division of arts became more pronounced. At the same time, though, general knowledge was still pretty limited compared to modern standards. Because of these limitations, people could be experts in many different fields at once. And this didn't just apply to artists! Even the general population was involved; as more was known and the general intellectual level of society increased, gentlemen, nobility, and courtiers of the day were expected to keep up with this rapidly growing cultural era. Expectations were high, and most members of the upper classes of society could sing or play a musical instrument and speak different languages, in addition to becoming skilled at their chosen professions.

Leonardo was considered one of the earliest Renaissance men because he not only studied a diversity of subjects, he became good at them, too. He wasn't just a dabbler in painting and architecture; he was a skilled designer who produced work that remains unrivaled even today. He was considered an expert in not just art, but also mathematics, invention, engineering, and construction. He was also clearly a talented writer; his own notebooks are one of our best sources of information about his life and career, as well as his ideas.

His inventions may seem primitive in light of modern technology and science, but for the Renaissance they were utterly astounding. What is most unusual is that his designs were advanced enough to have been innovative even 500 years later.

Is it possible to be a Renaissance man today? One thing's for sure: it's a lot harder in modern times. In addition to there simply being more people in the world, the world is also a much larger place due to technological advances as well as free trade and exchange. We're more aware of other cultures, and we have a much larger skill base. Today, people are also generally more knowledgeable, and, as a result, there's a lot more to know to become an expert in any particular field. To be a Renaissance architect, for example, you would have been apprenticed for a while before transitioning into doing your own projects. Today, architects must be licensed; while the process still requires a four-year internship, it also requires four years of graduate school beyond college! All these requirements make it difficult to be good at just one field, let alone several. Do you know anyone who is truly an expert at more than one thing? Sure, such people exist, but they're few and far between.

Leonardo was certainly one of the great painters of his day, but did he really have the same amount or level of competition that artists today have? There's no easy answer there—nor do we need one. Leonardo's work speaks for itself. Even today, his breadth and depth of knowledge would set him apart and given that, imagine what an astonishing figure he must have been 500 years ago! Suffice it to say that Leonardo was, in all respects, an original, and most likely would stand up well against any modern-day genius!

The real deal on *The Da Vinci Code*

Leonardo da Vinci has been a fascinating character for centuries, but he has achieved a new degree of popularity recently, with the publication of Dan Brown's wildly successful novel *The Da Vinci Code*. This novel takes the reader through a historical murder mystery, with clues placed throughout various artifacts including the Holy Grail and paintings such as the *Mona Lisa* and *The Last Supper*.

Of course, Brown's novel is just that—fiction. But many of the historical locations and works of art are real. This relationship to actual artworks and other artifacts has caused many people to question whether the whole story might also be real. Could there actually have been a conspiracy throughout the ages, and a secret society (of which Leonardo da Vinci himself was a member) charged with protecting secrets from Christianity's earliest days?

Leonardo would have been a prime candidate to leave historical clues to such a conspiracy, if it actually existed—he had a penchant for puzzles, a love of secrecy, and a superior intellect. Also, remember that the works of art, as well as the secret societies mentioned in the novel, do actually exist. But there's a world of difference between their mere existence and the likelihood that they were combined into a conspiracy.

True enough, the societies mentioned in the book, including the Priory of Sion, the Knights Templar, and Opus Dei, are real societies that exist in the real world. But their actual historical roles are quite different than the way they appear in the book. There is no evidence of any sort that these societies were involved in a plot to conceal the Holy Grail. And while scholars have analyzed da Vinci's *Mona Lisa* and other artists' works for centuries, looking for hidden codes or other secrets, they haven't found any.

Leonardo da Vinci certainly was interested in codes and mechanical devices, so it's possible he might have invented a message delivery device such as the cryptex mentioned in the book. But there is no historical evidence that he did so!

The secrets of Christianity *The Da Vinci Code* alludes to are controversial, to say the least. The novel suggests that the individual to the right of Jesus in Leonardo's painting of the "Last Supper" is actually Mary Magdalene, and this has been a popular notion over the years, especially in France because she is rumored to have gone there after Jesus's death and the Resurrection. While the Bible says nothing about Jesus and Mary Magdalene being lovers, the fact that these stories were prevalent during Leonardo's time may lend credence to Dan Brown's placement of Mary Magdalene in the story.

However, most art historians believe that the disciple in question is actually John, depicted in the androgynous form favored by Leonardo in this and other works (see number 88). Not only is there no evidence that Mary Magdalene was included in *The Last Supper*, it's unlikely that Leonardo was attempting any allusion to her body as the Holy Grail by including her and not a chalice in his painting. In recent years, the Catholic Church has finally put a stop to Mary Magdalene's wrongful portrayal as a prostitute, but there is still no concrete evidence proving that she and Jesus were ever married.

While much has been made of the supposed similarities between a self-portrait of Leonardo and The *Mona Lisa*, it's unlikely that Leonardo intentionally painted the famous work as a female self-portrait. More likely, da Vinci's painting and drawing style resulted in similar facial shapes and other characteristics between the *Mona Lisa* and his self-portraits, especially since a real historical woman is believed to have been the model (see number 38). There is no evidence in any of Leonardo's writings that he intended the *Mona Lisa* to be a representation of a union of male and female.

Another so-called secret mentioned in *The Da Vinci Code* has to do with the role of anagrams in the name of Leonardo's most famous painting. The title of the painting *Mona Lisa* is undeniably an anagram for *Amon L'Isa*; however, it is also an anagram for *Man As Oil*, and hundreds of other possibilities in various languages that Leonardo didn't even speak. In light of that, it's a stretch to think that Leonardo intended any reference to the ancient Egyptian mother and father gods—especially since there's little or no evidence that Leonardo had any knowledge of such mythology. Remember, Leonardo didn't have much of a formal education, and he probably never studied Egyptian deities.

So it's important to keep in mind that although works like *The Da Vinci Code* are fun escapes from reality, they're ultimately just fiction. Of course, the interest that Brown's novel has sparked in general art history (and, specifically, in Leonardo da Vinci) is certainly a good thing! Tourists hot on the trail of *The Da Vinci Code*, though, might be sorely disappointed not to find secret invisible-ink messages written in the Louvre. Nevertheless, the reward of seeing artwork like the *Mona Lisa* in person should be ample compensation in and of itself. Specifics of *The Da Vinci Code* aside, the Mona Lisa's smile is still as mysterious as anyone could ever want.

Da Vinci, Leonardo. *The Notebooks of Leonardo Da Vinci, Complete, Edition 9.* Translator Jean Paul Richter, 1888. Oxford, Mississippi: Project Gutenberg, 2001, 2002 by Michael S. Hart: *www.gutenberg.org/dirs/etext04/7ldvc09.txt* (accessed October 22, 2004).

Da Vinci, Leonardo. *The Notebooks of Leonardo Da Vinci, Complete, Edition 10.* Translator Jean Paul Richter, 1888. Oxford, Mississippi: Project Gutenberg, 2001, 2002 by Michael S. Hart: *www.gutenberg.org/dirs/etext04/8ldvc10.txt* (accessed October 22, 2004).

Freud, Sigmund. *Leonardo da Vinci and a Memory of His Childhood.* New York: W.W. Norton & Company, reissue edition, 1999.

Index